ATLANTIS
THE ANDES SOLUTION

D1375096

ATLANTIS
THE ANDES SOLUTION

The Discovery of South America
as the Legendary Continent of Atlantis
The Theory and the Evidence

J.M. ALLEN
Foreword by John Blashford-Snell

THE WINDRUSH PRESS · GLOUCESTERSHIRE

First published in Great Britain in 1998
by The Windrush Press
Little Window, High Street
Moreton-in-Marsh
Gloucestershire GL56 0LL

Telephone: 01608 652012
Fax: 01608 652125
Email: Windrush@Netcomuk.co.uk
Published in paperback, 1999

British Library Cataloguing-in-Publication Data
A catalogue record for this book is available from the British Library

ISBN 1 900624 25 7

Typeset by Carnegie Publishing Ltd, Lancaster
Printed and bound by Bookcraft (Bath) Ltd, Bath, Somerset, Great Britain

Cover design by Ariana Grabec-Dingman
The front of the jacket reproduces a detail of a statue from Tiahuanaco, Bolivia.
The background is an aerial photograph of abandoned irrigation plots northwest
of Lake Poopo, Bolivia

To order your free Windrush Press catalogue featuring all our titles, or to order please
Phone **01608 652012** or **01608 652025**
Fax **01608 652125**
email: Windrush@netcomuk.co.uk
Visit our web site: www.windrushpress.com
Write to us at
The Windrush Press
Little Window, High Street, Moreton-in-Marsh,
Gloucestershire GL56 0LL, UK

Dedication

If a dedication be required, then let it be to the people
of that Great Continent, presently called 'South America',
and formerly called:

ATLANTIS

.

The central figure on the Gateway to the Sun
in Tiahuanaco. He is depicted with eyes weeping tears,
originally inlaid with gold, and is said to be
crying for the sunken red land – Atlantis.[58]

Contents

	Foreword	ix
	Preface	1
1	Four Golden Keys to Atlantis	9
2	Condors over Atlantis	15
3	Plato's Account	29
4	Donnelly's Account	51
5	Atlantis, Crete and the Sea Peoples	59
6	Legacy of Aztlan	73
7	Land of the Four Quarters	81
8	Nature of Orichalcum	96
9	The Phoenician Navigators	106
10	Expedition Atlantis	121
11	Conclusion	131
	Satellite Photographs	136
	Last Thoughts	149
	Plato's Statements and a Commentary	151
	Source Books	164
	Acknowledgements	166
	Index	167

Until one is committed there is the chance to draw back; always ineffectiveness

Concerning all acts of initiative (and creation) there is one elementary truth, the ignorance of which kills countless ideas and splendid plans:—that the moment one definitely commits oneself, then providence moves too.

All sorts of things occur to help one that would not otherwise have occurred. A whole stream of events issues from the decision, raising in one's favour all manner of unforeseen incidents and meetings and material assistance which no man could have dreamed would come his way.

Whatever you can do or dream you can begin it. Boldness has genius, magic and power in it.

Begin it now.

GOETHE

Foreword

by Colonel John Blashford-Snell, OBE, DSc(Hon), FRSGS

ONE OF THE most intriguing mysteries of the world is the legend of Atlantis. Ever since Plato wrote of the City State and the disaster that befell it, scholars and explorers have sought to identify the site. Possible locations have been suggested in the Mediterranean, the Atlantic and the Gobi. Jim Allen has found a new area which seems to fit Plato's text. At over 12,000 feet in the Bolivian Altiplano he has identified a rectangular plain similar to Plato's description and examined what appears to be remains of a vast canal constructed by a pre-Inca culture.

His long and painstaking study of this fascinating subject has reinforced his opinions and I believe he has approached his research with an open mind and a determination to seek the truth. By using aerial photographs and checking the results on the ground, Jim has certainly found something. I leave it to the reader to judge whether this is indeed Plato's Atlantis, however I am confident that the remains of a hitherto unidentified culture may well be discovered in this region.

10 October 1996

Native chieftain whose body was daily covered in gold dust
which he washed off every evening in a mountain lake.

Preface

THE TELEPHONE RANG. It was the ninth call that morning. Another radio station, this time in Canada. Could I give them an interview? An article had appeared in *The Times* (20 February 1997) reviewing a theory I had put forward that a location on the Bolivian Altiplano in South America corresponded to the site of the lost civilisation of Atlantis.

The two most popular questions were, 'Why Bolivia?' and 'How did you come to find it?'

As to 'Why Bolivia?' I had to point out that it wasn't always called Bolivia. That was in fact a relatively modern name awarded to the country in 1825 after Simon Bolivar, the Great Liberator who freed the South American continent from Spanish rule, setting up independent countries such as Bolivia. Before that, Bolivia had formed part of the Spanish dominion of Alto Peru, the Spanish conquistadors effectively taking control of the country when they captured the last Inca emperor Atahualpa in 1532.

The Incas themselves governed the Andes for only a few hundred years, setting up a vast and efficient empire running the length of the Andes and themselves assimilating by conquest any tribes that stood in the way. Before them other empires had existed and even in their heyday the remains of the mysterious city of Tiahuanaco stood silent on the edge of Lake Titicaca, witness to a forgotten civilisation about which very little was known. Today Tiahuanaco stands about twenty miles from Lake Titicaca, but at one time it was on the edge of the lake and had harbour facilities as well as a central island surrounded by a moat or canal. The receding waters of the lake meant that an additional canal had subsequently to be dug to the lake, but the whole area is subject to climatic changes which alternate between severe droughts and extensive

1

flooding with subsequent damage to crops and fields. Local legend tells that the whole population was once destroyed in a flood and the later Incas claimed to have emerged from an island on Lake Titicaca after such a flood and gone forth to found the new empire centred on Cuzco.

We forget so easily, that 'America' is also a relatively modern name we have given to the entire continent. Before Columbus, the native peoples certainly didn't call it 'America'. In 1492, Christopher Columbus in an attempt to find a route by sea westwards to China or India made a landfall on an island called by the natives 'Guahani', which he promptly renamed San Salvador – present day Watling Island in what we now call the Bahamas or West Indies. On his third voyage in 1498 Columbus sailed along the coast of the mainland, passing through the Gulf of Paria near Trinidad then heading north-west, passing the Isle of Margarita before returning to his base at Haiti. On this voyage he was accompanied by Amerigo Vespucci who was later to return in a vessel commanded by Alonso de Hojeda who had got hold of a copy of Columbus' chart and followed the same route as Columbus but continued further westwards as far as Maracaibo. Seeing the houses there on stilts in the lake is said to have reminded Vespucci of Venice (Venezia) and thus this country came to be called Venezuela.[49]

On a later voyage made on behalf of Portugal, Vespucci sailed along the South American coastline past the River Plate as far as 50° south, thus establishing the land as a previously unknown continent. Vespucci was an experienced navigator, and developed a system of celestial navigation using the conjunction of the moon and a planet to calculate longitude.[54] In a letter which he wrote giving an account of his earlier voyage, he claimed to have visited the mainland of the 'New World' in 1497 – a year earlier than Columbus and when this was published in 1507, the European mapmaker Martin Waldseemuller proposed the South American continent be named in his honour, largely on account of Vespucci's recognition of the land as an unknown continent instead of a part of Asia as was previously thought. The name 'America' became popular and was later extended to the northern continent as well.[54]

But what was the native and/or what would be a more appropriate name for the whole continent? Before Columbus, maps existed which showed an island way out in the Atlantic Ocean opposite the Strait of Gibraltar. The 1455 map by Bartolomo Pareto

Map of 1455 by Bartolomeo Pareta (pre-Columbus) showing an island called Antillia.

shows this island as a large regular rectangle, but the name of the island is given as Antillia. (The islands of the Caribbean are still known today as the Greater and Lesser Antilles.) Sometimes it is said that Antillia consists of two words, 'illia' or 'ilha' (from the Portuguese) meaning 'island' and 'Ante' meaning 'before' suggesting that this was an island before the great continent. But there is a much more interesting possibility.

The whole of the South American continent has running along its length a mountain chain called the Andes – which is in fact a mispronunciation of 'Antis'.[50 & 59] And 'Antis' in the Quechua language of the Incas, means 'copper' and was also the name of the Indians who occupied the eastern slopes of the Andes mountains. Before the Conquest, a 'quarter' of the Inca empire was called Antisuyo – the kingdom of the Antis. So Antillia could perhaps more correctly be seen as the island of the Anti – a reference to both the people and the copper for which they were famous. It is said that exploitation of copper first began in the Americas where nuggets of pure copper could be found and it is sometimes said that nuggets of copper were the 'golden apples of the Hesperides' (according to myth, Mother Earth gave Hera a tree with golden apples, which was later guarded by the Hesperides in Hera's orchard on Mount Atlas, and Atlas according to the legend was none other than the first king of Atlantis.[39])

Another ancient name for the continent is 'Atlanta', said to be the Indian name before Columbus[51] but surely it is 'Atlantis' which is the most logical, combining Antis with 'Atl' which means water in the Mexican or Aztec Nahuatl tongue and the first inhabitants of both the Valley of Mexico and the High Altiplano lived in a watery environment where they created artificial watercourses, flooding areas of land and living on artificial islands; not only that but in the wet season vast areas of the Amazonian basin flood under water to a depth of some 30 ft. The earliest inhabitants (of Amazonia) lived permanently on rafts so surely no name could be more appropriate for the continent of South America than Plato's Atl-Antis or Atlantis.

As to the second question of how I came to identify the Altiplano as the site of Atlantis, it began when I began to take an interest in old monuments like Stonehenge, the Great Pyramid etc. I kept coming across references to ancient units of measurement such as the cubits and I could find no satisfactory explanation of what a cubit was, rejecting the facile explanation that it was merely the first recorded distance between the elbow and fingertip of some long-forgotten king.

So I launched into a massive study of all the ancient systems of measurement and discovered the true geodetic (Earth related) origins of all of them and found that they were all derived from either the diameter or circumference of the planet Earth upon which we live, units such as the English inch and foot, the Egyptian cubits of the Pyramid, Ezekiel's cubits of the Temple and the Sumerian cubits of ancient Mesopotamia being related in this way.

But, in the study if the cubits, I also came across such units as the Greek foot and the Greek cubit and then, in turn, the Greek stade which was said to have been 1/10 th of a minute of latitude and a unit of measurement known to the ancient Egyptians and built into the apothem or sloping side of the Great Pyramid. Then came Plato's story of Atlantis with its description of a rectangular plain which he said existed in the centre of the lost continent, and of course the measurements since he said the plain measured 3,000 × 2,000 stades. The plain was according to Plato, surrounded by a vast perimeter canal 1 stade wide, which ran right around the edge of the plain, a distance of 10,000 stades and the plain supported a system of lateral canals at intervals of 100 stades and transverse canals also at distances of presumably 100 stades so the whole system is envisaged as a vast rectangular-shaped chequerboard pattern.

Having variously read that America might be the continent of Atlantis, it seemed to me that if that were so, then somewhere on the continent of America there would have to be a place where the rectangular plain would fit in.

So I began a systematic search of the Americas, looking for a place where the rectangular grid of canals would fit in, bearing in mind according to Plato it also had to be 'in the centre of the whole island'. Only one location seemed appropriate and that was the Altiplano, or rather the portion of the Altiplano adjacent to Lake Poopo for that was where the rectangular-shaped part of the Altiplano lay. In the beginning it wasn't so apparent that it was rectangular at all, for at that time large portions of the map I held were blank, unsurveyed areas. And the region appeared to be only half of Plato's required dimension suggesting a stade equal to half a Greek stade, i.e. 300 ft instead of 600 ft, but it was in the correct proportion. One must also not forget Plato himself emphasised that Greek names were not the originals but were given in his story 'only to make it more agreeable to his readers'.

It was when I decided to build a three dimensional model of the Altiplano that the rectangular nature of the plain became fully apparent, for then I had to cut out each 1,000 ft contour, building up the model layer by layer and thus I found the 'rectangular plain enclosed by mountains'. Then other pieces began to fit. I acquired extra translations of Plato's text, each translation contributing perhaps a line or a word which clarified the mystery such as Lee's footnote that the plain lay midway along the greatest length of the continent – so it was clear the continent was South America and not all of the Americas. In addition the translation by Donnelly says Atlantis disappeared in a single day and night of earthquakes, floods and *rain* – his being the only translation to mention rain – which in the enclosed basin of the Altiplano would certainly result in flooding.

But did the story really being here? And what was the true background which led to the discovery?

True I had always had a remote, romantic interest in South America, but that dated back to very early days and was in company of adventurous reading particularly of such dreams as sailing around the world in small ships. But at the age of eighteen I had joined the Royal Air Force, and following on from my love of geography and photography in particular had joined as what was then called a 'Plotter Air Photo' – which meant plotting the areas covered by aerial photos onto maps and charts of various scales.

So for me I guess, the air force became my university. I embarked on my training course where being young and enthusiastic I gained a previously unheard of 99 per cent for the mock exam and 98 per cent for the actual exam – at least for the theory side and I was able to indulge in all the sporting activities which people notoriously join the Forces for, including fencing, rowing, dinghy sailing in Cyprus and riding including playing polo in Malta.

By that time I had progressed to being a Photographic Interpreter which meant studying aerial photos to see what information could be extracted from them, and of course it meant being an expert in maps and map scales and such calculations as to how long an object would be on the ground if it measured a certain distance on a photo.

At the time of leaving the RAF I owned and lived upon a large motor cruiser which I sailed along the English waterways until I arrived at Cambridge where I began working as a cartographer for a public utility. But it was the RAF training which enabled me to identify which maps I would require to check out Plato's statements relative to the Altiplano and I became a frequent visitor to Stanford's map shop in London. And it was the RAF training which allowed me to construct a topographical model of the entire Altiplano and also one of the whole continent, then later to acquire through a private agency the required Landsat photos from orbiting satellites in order to extend my search by looking for any evidence of the city or remains of the canal which could be found on site.

And what appeared to be part of Plato's canal could be seen on those early photos. But it was never really clear that it was a canal. The scale of the material was so small as to preclude absolutely positive identification, but there was something there, yet again at the same time someone suggested there were no canals, merely 'fault lines'. In any event, even if it turned out to be only a natural fault, it still carried water and was of the same immense dimension Plato quoted, so would it not be one coincidence too many that a fault or feature (or canal?) similar to Plato's description should exist in this remote desert. A natural fault would still not invalidate the theory since Plato said the features of the plain were '*as a result of natural forces*, together with the labours of many kings' so perhaps a natural feature could have inspired the construction or continuation of a canal elsewhere, and the mainstay of the theory was not the canal but the rectangular plain itself.

It was evident, however, that at some time the canal or feature would have to be visited on the ground; little did I imagine that many years would go by before someone first visited the site on the ground or that that person would be myself. But, as someone from NASA once wrote to me, he agreed that a canal system might exist on the Altiplano although he would be surprised if it should be 600 ft wide (Plato's measurement) but if it should be true, what a great discovery! And that, as he said, 'Is why we torture ourselves' – in other words, we have to know!

Who then can resist the possibility that here after all lies the remains of the fabulous city described by Plato, beneath the sands of the remote desert bordering Lake Poopo, a possible contribution to lost knowledge which as a writer in the *London Evening Standard* once considered 'Could lead to one of the greatest intellectual revolutions since the time of Charles Darwin', a city of golden roofs and palaces with treasures surpassing those of Tutankamun, the splendours of Egypt, Knossos or Troy and walls and temples plated with the Gold of Atlantis.

Please note that the superscript numbers in the text refer to the Source Books on pages 164–5.

CHAPTER 1

Four Golden Keys to Atlantis

PERHAPS ONE OF the greatest unsolved mysteries of our time is the site of the lost island of Atlantis.

The history of the island of Atlantis was written by the Greek philosopher Plato around 380 BC. Plato in his books *Critias* and *Timaeus* said that the island of Atlantis was a continent as large as Asia and Libya combined, but, in a single day and night of disastrous rain followed by earthquakes and floods, the island of Atlantis sank into the sea and disappeared.

Apparently the island was situated in the Atlantic Ocean in front of the straits called by the Greeks 'the Pillars of Hercules' (the Strait of Gibraltar) and here we have the root of the problem, for in accordance with our modern geological science it is said to be not possible for a whole continent to sink and disappear in the space of a single day; no one has ever found any remains of a civilisation or continent sunk in the Atlantic and many people, especially archaeologists, don't believe in the truth of Plato's story.

Another factor which has greatly influenced the archaeologists is that there is a huge amount of science fiction books and films on Atlantis which includes material on electric submarines and crystal death ray machines and the like, and this has brought a large element of fantasy and discredit to the subject.

But if anyone takes the time and trouble to read Plato's texts for himself, it is obvious that there are no submarines or crystal machines or things of this type in Plato's work. There is nothing more than a very extensive and detailed geographic description of the continent which existed on the other side of the Atlantic Ocean and, with the knowledge and resources we have today like satellite mapping technology, it is very obvious that the land called by Plato 'Atlantis' is the same which today we call 'South America'.

To begin with, the word 'Atlantis' consists of two native South American words, 'Atl' which means 'water' in the native tongue and 'Antis' which means 'copper', origin of the name of the Andes mountains and the name of a tribe which still lives today in a part of Peru. For the Incas, their empire was called 'Tahuantinsuyo' – land of the four quarters – and one of these quarters was 'Antisuyo', homeland of the Antis Indians.

The native Aztecs claimed to have come from an island originally called 'Aztlan': their own language was called Nahu*atl*, they had many words such as Tam*atl* (tomato), Chocol*atl* (chocolate) and Quetzalco*atl*, their principal god. Also in Mexico there are many sites with names such as Cuic*atlan*, Miahu*atlan* and Maz*atlan*.

But the key to the mystery is the description given by Plato of a plain which existed in the centre of the continent. This plain was in the centre of the continent but at the same time was next to the ocean, further it was in the centre of the longest side of the continent, the plain was very smooth and level, it was surrounded by mountains on all sides, it was in a region very high above the level of the ocean and the plain had the form of 'a quadrangle, rectilinear for the most part and elongated'.

We can be certain that this is also a perfect description of the Bolivian Altiplano, the largest perfectly level plain in the world and which also contains the two inland seas of Lake Titicaca and Lake Poopo. But the part which interests us is the part surrounding Lake Poopo because this is the part which has the unique rectangular shape and the presence of the inland sea is the second key to the mystery.

Plato said that on the plain there was a city which was also an island and had the name of 'Atlantis'. It was built on the remains of an extinct volcano and consisted of a central island surrounded by alternate rings of water and land. Now Plato always maintained that the story of Atlantis was not an invention of his own but came originally from the priests of the Egyptian temples.

Now suppose that in the translation there should be an error so fundamental and simple as this; it was not the island *continent* of Atlantis which sank into the sea in a single day but only the island *city* of Atlantis which disappeared under the huge inland sea of Lake Poopo.

Plato himself did not know anything of the Bolivian Altiplano or of the continents of the 'Americas' and thought that the sunken continent was exactly in front of the entrance to the Mediterranean because he said that the ocean in those parts was no longer navigable 'on account of the barrier of shallow mud which the island threw up as it settled down' and which 'prevents those who are sailing out from here to the ocean beyond from proceeding further'. But in truth it is not the Atlantic Ocean which is no longer navigable but only the shallow Lake Poopo which only reaches a depth of a few feet and in the dry season has been known to dry up altogether leaving behind brilliant white salt deposits.

The third key to the mystery is that we should note the island disappeared in a single day and night of *rain*, which resulted in earthquakes and floods. This region is in the centre of the Avenue of Volcanoes, it is a region where there are always earthquakes and floods – the plain is like a closed basin and should there be a period of torrential rain there would be no possibility of exit for the water from the plain. In fact, thousands of years ago, the entire Altiplano was the bed of a gigantic inland sea, known as Lake Minchin for the period between 38,000 and 23,000 BC and re-named Lake Tauca for the period when it reappeared between 9,000 and 8,000 BC.

With this new hypothesis, it is clear that all the other details given by Plato belong here.

The walls of the city and temples were covered with metals which we today consider rare and precious such as gold, silver, copper, tin and another mysterious metal called 'orichalcum' which could be polished and 'sparkled like red fire'. Here we have the fourth key to the site of the city. All these metals are found not far from Lake Poopo. The city of Oruro has the mining industry as its base, in Corocoro there are mines of gold and copper, Potosi was the mountain of solid silver which became the fountain of wealth for the Spanish empire and today is the mountain famous for its deposits of tin. Orichalcum was most probably an alloy of gold and copper and occurs as a natural alloy only in the Andes Mountains; Plato mentioned that it was a natural alloy since it was *mined* in many places in the island.

The tradition of covering the walls of cities and temples in gold and silver was continued by the Incas who also had a fabulous garden full of birds and animals all made of solid gold. Other similarities – the Incas constructed baths where they used the natural springs of hot and cold water, they kept statues in solid gold in the images of their ancestors and said that the first inhabitants of the land were born in pairs just as Plato claimed for Atlantis.

One of the other interesting aspects of Plato's text is the description of a huge system of irrigation canals which the kings of Atlantis had constructed on the plain. One of today's problems is that for the most of the year there is no rainfall and because of this the ground has reverted to desert. At other times in January, February and March there are floods and when the water later evaporates it leaves behind deposits of salt which contaminate the land.

According to Plato the kings of Atlantis had constructed a canal of such dimensions 'It seems incredible that it should be so large as the account states but we must report what we heard . . . its width was one stade (600 ft)' and this canal went right round the perimeter of the entire plain, collecting the streams from the mountains and discharging them into the sea somewhere in the vicinity of the city. Additional canals of 100 ft in width were cut across the plain at intervals of 100 stades, discharging into the large canal on the seaward side of the plain and connected to each other by further transverse passages. It was in this manner, it was said, they transported the timbers from the mountains to the city, also the fruits of the earth of which they harvested two crops per year, making use of the rains from Heaven in the winter and the waters that issue from the earth in summer, redistributed by means of the extensive canal system.

In the whole of the world it is very probably that there exists no other plain so level, with this particular rectangular configuration and with the resources of water in the surrounding mountains including the immense reserve of pure fresh water in Lake Titicaca to the north. Additionally, if one follows for example the 12,000 ft elevation contour on a map of the Altiplano, one can see that it would be possible to construct a canal which would run around the perimeter of the rectangular plain making a circuit which returns to itself in the manner described by Plato.

It only remains then to discover on site evidence of a channel 600 ft wide to say without any more doubts that here indeed is the proof that the city and civilisation of Atlantis existed in these parts.

With satellite and aerial photos, it is possible to say yes, there are signs of a massive canal in a region just north-west of Lake

Poopo. In July of 1995 I travelled personally to the Altiplano where I hired a jeep and drove into the desert to investigate this particular site. I found the remains of a channel of enormous dimensions, the base of the canal was around 120 ft wide and the gently sloping sides were each of some 230 ft making just under 600 ft from crest to crest of the parallel embankments. The channel was built in this manner because the soft, sandy material of the construction dictated gentle slopes yet at the same time since the embankments were raised perhaps 25 ft above the level of the plain, the water would gravity feed onto the plain when the channel was full. The base of the channel was also about 25 ft below the level of the plain so at other times when the plain was flooded in the wet season it would act as a relief drainage channel dispersing the waters to other areas.

Now how is it possible that the history of Atlantis existed only in the writings of Plato and at what period did it disappear?

Plato said that the story came originally from Egypt at a time when the empire of Atlantis (which controlled all of North Africa and the Mediterranean up to Italy) was engaged in a war of conquest against Egypt and the Greeks. Here again Plato committed an error because he gave the same date for the foundation of the civilisation of Atlantis as he gave for its destruction, i.e. 9,000 years before his time and it is certain that a civilisation cannot be founded and destroyed in the same day!

According to our archaeologists there were no civilisations anywhere in the world in the period 9,000 years before Plato, yet it is interesting that indeed the Altiplano was flooded and reverted to an inland sea at this time.

However if the 9,000 'years' were in effect 9,000 lunar months in accordance with the lunar calendar then the period for the end of Atlantis would be the years more or less around 1200 BC and at this time, specifically in 1220 and 1186 BC there were huge invasions of Egypt by a people called 'the Sea Peoples' or 'the people who came from the isles in the midst of the sea'.

The invaders consisted of a confederation of nations. It is also interesting that, as one can see from the bas-reliefs on the walls of the temple of Medinet Habu in Egypt, their ships were sailing ships without oars and in the narrow confines of the Nile Delta they were totally defeated by the powerful Rameses III. Thousands of the invaders were taken prisoner and later given their own lands to settle, such as the Philistines who were allowed to occupy the land which took their name and became Palestine.

Others entered into the service of the Egyptian king and it seems very likely that the true history of Atlantis, with so many precise details of a geographic nature, originated with one of these.

Captured Philistine warrior
with distinctive headgear,
one of the 'Sea Peoples'
defeated by Rameses III.

CHAPTER 2

Condors over Atlantis

THE ANSWER to the question 'Where is Atlantis' is very simple – it is exactly where Plato said it was – 'At a distant point in the Atlantic Ocean', 'In front of the mouth of the Strait of Gibraltar' (translation R. G. Bury) or again 'Opposite the Strait of Gibraltar' (translation Desmond Lee). Atlantis was a continent and there is only one continent opposite the Strait of Gibraltar – presently called 'America'.

The continental mainland was first sighted by Christopher Columbus on Wednesday 1 August 1498 and he gave it the name of Isla Santa, believing it to be an island.[55] The Portuguese similarly mistook it for an island at first, calling it 'the Island of Santa Cruz'. This is the land which Plato called Atlantis and today we simply call *South America*.

To begin with, the island was of a size comparable to Libya and Asia combined. From it one could cross to the other islands and from these, to the whole of the continent encompassing the veritable ocean. By this, the continent encompassing the ocean, is meant the continuous continental land mass of Asia/Europe/Africa.

Okeanos was to the Greeks an all-embracing water encircling the Earth and in it, America can be seen not only as a continent but as an island. We can further conclude that in all probability Plato specifically meant South America, itself a continent in its own right, since he later continues . . .

'Bordering on the sea and extending through the centre of the whole island there was a plain'. The translation by Lee adds the footnote 'i.e. midway along its greatest length'.

This plain is the Altiplano, it is in the centre of the 'island', midway along its longest side and is at the same time next to the sea, meaning the Pacific Ocean.

15

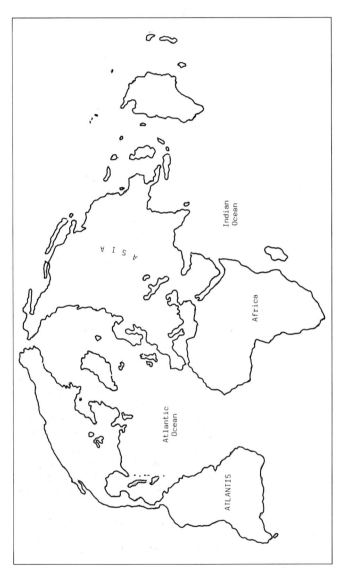

Modern map projection showing Atlantis opposite the Strait of Gibraltar.

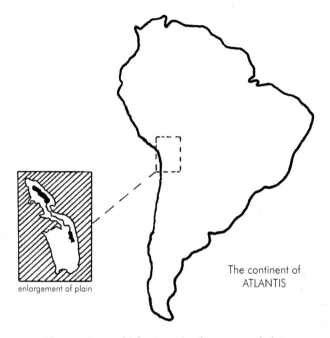

enlargement of plain

The continent of
ATLANTIS

The continent of Atlantis and enlargement of plain.

Taking the length of the plain from the shores of Lake Titicaca to its southern boundary at Cordilleria de Lipez is a distance of 600 kms. Near the centre of this elongated plain is the site of the low mountain that was destined to become first the dwelling of Poseidon and later, the city of Atlantis, now submerged under Lake Poopo. Here is the sea that is 'Impassable and unsearchable, being blocked up by the shoal mud which the island created as it settled down'. Lake Poopo, a salty inland sea over fifty miles long remains a shallow sea only a few feet deep and is sometimes known to dry up altogether.

Poseidon was the founder of Atlantis, which he received as his allotment when the Gods were dividing up the Earth. He married the daughter of one of the natives, who lived on the mountain already mentioned.

And when this damsel was now come to marriageable age, her mother died and also her father; and Poseidon, being smitten with desire for her, wedded her; and to make the hill whereon she dwelt impregnable he broke it off all round about; and he made circular belts of land and sea enclosing one another alternately, some greater, some smaller, two being of land and three of sea, which he carved as it were out of the midst of the island; and these belts were at even distances on all sides, so as to be impassable for man; for at that time neither ships nor sailing were as yet in existence.

The entire region surrounding the Altiplano is volcanic with hot and cold springs and the plain is abundantly studded with volcanic outcrops. Any such outcrop or dormant volcanic cone could easily be turned into an island by flooding the adjacent plain.

And Poseidon himself set in order with ease, as a god would, the central island, bringing up from beneath the earth two springs of waters, the one flowing warm from its source, the other cold, and producing out of the earth all kinds of food in plenty. And he begat five pairs of twin sons and reared them up; and when he had divided all the island of Atlantis into ten portions, he assigned to the first born of the eldest sons his mother's dwelling and the allotment surrounding it, which was the largest and the best; and him he appointed to be king over the rest, and the others to be rulers, granting to each the rule over many men and a large tract of country. And to all of them he gave names, giving to him that was eldest and king the name after which the whole island was called and the sea spoken of as the Atlantic, because the first king who then reigned had the name of Atlas. And the name of his younger twin-brother, who had for his portion the extremity of the island near the pillars of Heracles up to the part of the country now called Gadeira after the name of that region, was Eumelus in Greek, but in the native tongue Gadeirus – which fact may have given its title to the country.

. . . So all these, themselves and their descendants, dwelt for many generations bearing rule over many other islands throughout the sea, and holding sway besides, over the Mediterranean peoples as far as Egypt and Tuscany.

Now a large family of distinguished sons sprang from Atlas; but it was the eldest, who, as king, always passed on the sceptre to the eldest of his sons, and thus they preserved the sovereignty for many generations; and the wealth they possessed was so immense that the like had never been seen before in any royal house nor will ever easily be seen again; and they were provided with everything of which provision was needed either in the city or throughout the rest of the country. For because of their headship they had a large supply of imports from abroad, and the island itself furnished most of the requirements of daily life – metals, to begin with, both the hard kind and the fusible kind, which are extracted by mining, and also that kind which is now known only by name but was more than a name then, there being mines of it in many places of the island – I mean 'orichalcum', which was the most precious of the metals then known, except gold.

It brought forth also in abundance all the timbers that a forest provides for the labours of carpenters; and of animals it produced a sufficiency, both of tame and wild. Moreover it contained a very large stock of elephants; for there was an ample food supply not only for all the other animals which haunt the marshes and lakes and rivers, or the mountains or the plains, but likewise also for this animal, which of its nature is the largest and most voracious. And in addition to all this, it produced and brought to perfection all those sweet-scented stuffs which the earth produces now, whether made of roots or herbs or trees, or liquid gums derived from flowers or fruits. The cultivated fruit also, and the dry, which serves us for nutriment, and all the other kinds that we use for our meals – the various species of which are comprehended under the name 'vegetables' – and all the produce of trees which affords liquid and solid food and unguents, and the fruit of the orchard trees, so hard to store, which is grown for the sake of amusement and pleasure, and all the after-dinner fruits that we serve up as welcome remedies for the sufferer from repletion – all these that hallowed island, as it lay then beneath the sun, produced in marvellous beauty and endless abundance.

Atlantis the continent was, according to Plato, a confederation of ten kings. These kings held a tremendous power which extended to Europe as far as Italy and Africa as far as Libya. Although the island was self-sufficient in metals, fruits and the general necessities of life, because of the leadership of these kings they also maintained a supply of imports from abroad.

A country rich in minerals, South America is amply stocked with timbers, roots, herbs, gums, flowers, fruits and all in 'endless abundance'. What better description of the tropical jungle? The landscape is likewise varied with mountains, plains, marshes, lakes and rivers. Even the elephant is not out of place since the remains of mastodons have been found [11] which were at one time hunted with the spear, and in the Argentinian Pampas no less a person than Charles Darwin found the remains of horses,[26] an animal which was unknown to the Indians at the time of the Spanish Conquest.

> And thus, receiving from the earth all these products, they furnished forth their temples and royal dwellings, their harbours and their docks, and all the rest of their country, ordering all in the fashion following.
>
> First of all they bridged over the circles of sea which surrounded the ancient metropolis, making thereby a road towards and from the royal palace. Beginning at the sea, they bored a channel right through to the outermost circle, and thus they made the entrance to it from the sea like that to a harbour by opening out a mouth large enough for the greatest ships to sail through. Moreover, through the circles of land, which divided those of sea, they opened out a channel leading from circle to circle, large enough to give passage to a single trireme; and this they roofed over so that the sea-way was subterranean, for the lips of the land-circles were raised a sufficient height above the level of the sea.

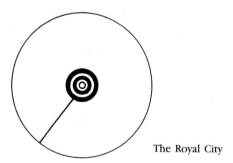

The Royal City

The greatest of the circles into which a boring was made for the sea was three stades in breadth, and the circle of land next to it was of equal breadth; and of the second pair of circles that of water was two stades in breadth and that of dry land equal again to the preceding one of water; and the circle which ran round the central island itself was of a stade's breadth. And this island, wherein stood the royal palace, was of five stades in diameter.

And the stone they quarried from beneath the central island all round, and from beneath the outer and inner circles, some of it being white, some black and some red; and while quarrying it they constructed two inner docks, hollowed out and roofed over by the native rock . . . And they covered with brass as though with a plaster, all of the circumference of the wall which surrounded the outermost circle; and that of the inner one they coated with tin; and that which encompassed the acropolis itself with orichalcum which sparkled like fire.

Such then was the state of things round about the abode of the kings. And after crossing the three outer harbours, one found a wall which began at the sea and ran round in a circle, at a uniform distance of fifty stades from the largest circle and harbour, and its ends converged at the seaward end of the channel. The whole of this wall had numerous houses built on to it, set close together; while the sea-way and the largest harbour were filled with ships and merchants coming from all quarters, which by reason of their multitude caused clamour and tumult of every description and an unceasing din night and day.

The red or black stone quarried from beneath the central island is typical of a volcanic region and the size of the city complex, 27 stades, is representative of a typical volcano found on the plain. In the island city was a temple to Poseidon and this was overlaid with gold, silver, and orichalcum. Brass is a mixture of copper and zinc whereas bronze is an alloy of copper and tin and orichalcum an alloy of copper and one other, unknown metal, probably gold and probably also a natural alloy since there were 'mines of it in many places of the island'.

So the four principal metals were gold, silver, copper and tin, all in sufficient quantities to plate the walls and temples.

Bolivia has the largest silver deposits in the world and its main export is tin. It is also rich in gold, copper, lead, zinc, antimony and wolfram. Many mines produce more than one metal and sometimes as many as four metals are found occurring naturally together. Potosi with its legendary mountain of silver was at one time a by-word for a fabulous untold wealth and is now famous for its mountain of solid tin. Tin, although neither rare nor precious is unique in that it is not found in very many places of the world, and there can be very few places indeed where it is found in the company of so many other desirable metals. This mining region straddles a river system (the Pilcomayo) which discharges some 1500 miles distant in the Rio de la Plata, which actually means 'river of silver'. Atlantis was a maritime power and the Pilcomayo was also the route to the Altiplano. Regarding the Altiplano, it would be hard to improve on Plato's words . . .

Profile through the centre of the plain.

> In the first place, then, according to the account, the whole region rose sheer out of the sea to a great height, but the part about the city was all a smooth plain, enclosing it round about, and being itself encircled by mountains which stretched as far as to the sea; and this plain had a level surface and was as a whole rectangular in shape, being 3,000 stades long on either side and 2,000 stades wide at its centre, reckoning upwards from the sea.

This is the southern part of the Altiplano and is the level plain, rectangular in shape, adjoining the inland sea of Lake Poopo. This part of the plain forms a basin within the plateau stretching right up to Lake Titicaca and this basin is encircled by mountains which 'stretch as far as to the sea' – meaning the Pacific Ocean and its width, as Plato says, is 2,000 stades 'reckoning upwards from the sea', the sea here being Lake Poopo.

Solon recovered the original sense of the story from the Egyptian writings and in order to make it more acceptable to his readers, substituted familiar Greek names such as Trireme and Stade. The stade here is therefore not a Greek stadium but a 'half-stade' of 300 ft, the important point being that the plain is rectangular in the *ratio* of 3,000 : 2,000 of these units.

The next part of the story is indeed the most incredible and

The level, rectangular plain encircled by mountains which stretch as far as to the sea.

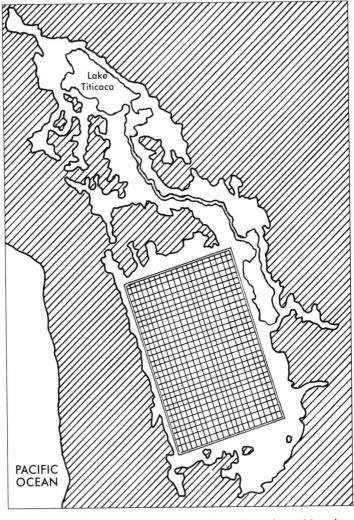

The irrigated plain of 3,000 × 2,000 stades with canals at 100 stade intervals.

certainly the most important, since it contains the key to the whole mystery of Atlantis.

> Now as a result of natural forces, together with the labours of many kings which extended over many ages, the condition of the plain was this. It was originally a quadrangle, rectilinear for the most part and elongated, and what it lacked of this shape they made right by means of a trench dug round about it. Now as regards the depth of this trench and its breadth and length, it seems incredible that it should be so large as the account states, considering that it was made by hand, and in addition to all the other operations, but none the less we must report what we heard; it was dug out to a depth of a plethrum and to a uniform breadth of a stade, and since it was dug round the whole of the plain its consequent length was 10,000 stades. It received the streams which came down from the mountains and after circling round the plain, and coming towards the city on this side and on that, it discharged them thereabouts into the sea. And on the inland side of the city channels were cut in straight lines, of about 100 ft in width, across the plain, and these discharged themselves into the trench on the seaward side, the distance between each being 100 stades. It was in this way that they conveyed to the city the timber from the mountains and transported also on boats the seasons' products, by cutting transverse passages from one channel to the next and also to the city. And they cropped the land twice a year, making use of the rains from Heaven in the winter, and the waters that issue from the earth in summer, by conducting the streams from the trenches.

When we read that the trench surrounding the plain had a uniform breadth of a stade, we must realise that the reason for this massive trench was not primarily to facilitate plying craft, but to accommodate the volume of water that was needed to irrigate the plain. In other words, we are talking about a huge irrigation scheme which enclosed an area of over *12 million acres*.

By carefully planning this trench to follow the contours of the land around the perimeter of the plain, the waters from the mountains could be brought down to Lake Poopo, and thence, via the smaller trenches at 100 stade intervals, across the length and breadth of the entire plain. The digging of the perimeter trench and cross trenches is no mean achievement, but it should be borne in mind that these trenches would be of 'V' shaped profile, thus reducing the amount of material removed.

Some archaeologists hold that this entire plain may once have been the bed of an inland sea, but now the soil consists of a mixture of black volcanic ash, red sandstone and clay, which can be packed hard giving the appearance of rock yet easily broken up in the hand to join the fine dust swept down by the mountain winds.

Large areas of the plain adjoining Lake Poopo consist of dried-up salt pans. This region is arid, with only five inches of rainfall per year. Yet to the north is a vast body of fresh water – Lake Titicaca. With a surface area of 3,500 square miles fed by twenty-five moun-

tain streams, Lake Titicaca is the highest navigable lake in the world. It is 140 miles long with a maximum depth of 1500 ft and according to local tradition is the home of the sun god who created the first men, and later the birthplace of the first Inca, the son of the sun.

At one time Lake Titicaca had a much higher water level than it has today,[6] as may be evidenced by water marks around the edge of the lake. To the south of the lake, the water fed a river (the Desaguadero) which flowed first to Lake Poopo then down the entire length of the plain.

Today, Lake Titicaca is receding, and the valuable waters mostly soak away beneath the plain. Some of the fresh water is still carried by the River Desaguadero down to the choked-up Lake Poopo

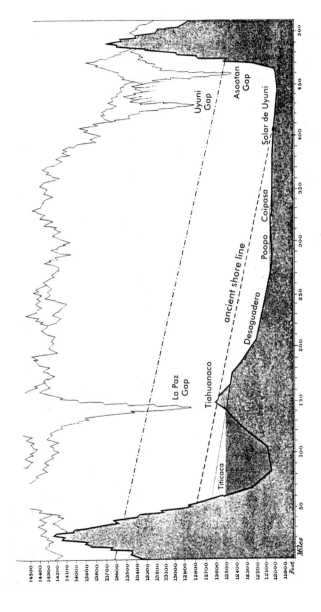

Exaggerated elevational section through Altiplano showing ancient shore lines. Note the slant caused by rise of land at northern end. Source: *Built Before the Flood*, H. S. Bellamy.

where, finding no further outlet, it eventually dissipates, leaving behind the mineral salts which become concentrated in the lake. In the wet season, Lake Poopo quickly overflows, running down an old irrigation canal and across the level plain. Large areas are flooded and when the water gradually evaporates or filters away, the salt is left behind in large pans called *Salars*. The Salar de Coipasa and Salar de Uyuni cover areas of 700 and 3,500 square miles respectively.

The whole Altiplano is an enclosed basin and although the canal system could disperse the waters in normal times, a period of torrential rainfall could have disastrous results turning the whole area into a gigantic inland sea.

> One grievous day and night befell them . . . there occurred portentous earthquakes and floods . . . the island of Atlantis was swallowed up by the sea and vanished.

Mayan glyph showing the Flood, volcanic eruption
and a city falling into the sea.

══ CHAPTER 3 ══

Plato's Account

THE ORIGINAL SOURCE of the story of Atlantis lies in two books by Plato: *Timaeus* reference 20E–25D and *Critias* reference 108E–121C (Plato Vol IX).

The complete account is given here so that readers may avail themselves of the entire text without alteration or omission.

Plato claimed that the story originated in Egypt, where it was given to a visiting Greek statesman, Solon. From Solon it devolved to Critias, who kept it in writing and recounted it at the festival of Athena. In *Timaeus* the story is introduced by Critias and given the form of a lecture by the Egyptian priest to Solon. In *Critias*, the tale is continued by Critias himself.

The translation is that by the Rev. R. G. Bury, reproduced by kind permission of LOEB Classical Library, Harvard University Press.

An alternative and later translation is that by Desmond Lee, published by Penguin Books.

Timaeus 20E–25D

The story opens when a discussion takes place as to the origin and antiquity of mankind. One of the speakers, Critias, recounts a tale of ancient Athens and how they defeated an invading army which was attempting to enslave the whole of the Mediterranean. That army was the royal army of Atlantis.

LISTEN then, Socrates, to a tale which, though passing strange, is yet wholly true, as Solon, the wisest of the Seven, once upon a time declared. Now Solon – as indeed he often says himself in his poems – was a relative and very dear friend of our great-grandfather

Dropides; and Dropides told our grandfather Critias – as the old man himself, in turn, related to us – that the exploits of this city in olden days, the record of which perished through time and the destruction of its inhabitants, were great and marvellous, the greatest of all being one which it would be proper for us now to relate both as a payment of our debt of thanks to you and also as a tribute to praise, chanted as it were duly and truly, in honour of the Goddess on this her day of festival.

Socrates – Excellent! But come now, what was this exploit described by Critias, following Solon's report, as a thing not verbally recorded, although actually performed by this city long ago?

Critias – I will tell you: it is an old tale, and I heard it from a man not young. For indeed at that time, as he said himself, Critias was already close upon ninety years of age, while I was somewhere about ten; and it chanced to be that day of the Apaturia which is called 'Cureotis'. The ceremony for boys which was always customary at the feast was held also on that occasion, our fathers arranged contests in recitation. So while many poems of many poets were acclaimed, since the poems of Solon were at that time new, many of us children chanted them. And one of our fellow tribesmen – whether he really thought so at the time or whether he was paying a compliment to Critias – declared that in his opinion Solon was not only the wisest of men in all else, but in poetry also he was of all poets the noblest. Whereat the old man (I remember the scene well) was highly pleased and said with a smile, 'If only, Amynander, he had not taken up poetry as a byplay but had worked hard at it like others, and if he had completed the story he brought here from Egypt, instead of being forced to lay it aside owing to the seditions and all the other evils he found here on his return – why then, I say, neither Hesiod nor Homer nor any other poet would ever have proved more famous than he.'

'And what was the story, Critias?' said the other.

'Its subject,' replied Critias, 'Was a very great exploit, worthy indeed to be accounted to be the most notable of all exploits, which was performed by this city, although the record of it has not endured until now owing to lapse of time and the destruction of those who wrought it.'

'Tell us from the beginning', said Amynander, 'What Solon related and how, and who were the informants who vouched for its truth.'

'In the Delta of Egypt,' said Critias, 'Where, at its head, the stream of the Nile parts in two, there is a certain district called the Saitic.

The chief city in this district is Sais – the home of King Amasis – the founder of which, as they say, was a goddess whose Egyptian name is Neith, and in Greek, as they assert, Athena. These people profess to be great lovers of Athens and in a measure akin to our people here. And Solon said that when he travelled there he was held in great esteem amongst them; moreover, when he was questioning such of their priests as were most versed in ancient lore about their ancient history, he discovered that neither he himself nor any other Greek knew anything at all, one might say, about such matters. And, on one occasion, when he wished to draw them on to discourse on ancient history, he attempted to tell them the most ancient of our traditions, concerning Phoroneus, who was said to be the first man, and Niobe; and he went on to tell the legend about Deucalion and Pyrra after the flood, and how they survived it, and to give the genealogy of their descendants; and by recounting the number of years occupied by the events mentioned he tried to calculate the periods of time. Whereupon one of the priests, a prodigiously old man, said, 'O Solon, Solon, you Greeks are always children; there is not such a thing as an old Greek.' And on hearing this he asked, 'What mean you by this saying?' And the priest replied, 'You are young in soul, every one of you. For therein you possess not a single belief that is ancient and derived from old tradition, nor yet one science that is hoary with age. And this is the cause thereof: There have been and there will be many and divers destructions of mankind, of which the greatest are by fire and water, and lesser ones by countless other means. For in truth the story that is told in your country as well as ours, how once upon a time, Phaethon, son of Helios, yoked his father's chariot, and, because he was unable to drive it along the course taken by his father, burnt up all that was upon the earth, and himself perished by a thunderbolt – that story, as it is told, has the fashion of a legend, but the truth of it lies in the occurrence of a shift of the bodies in the heavens which move round the earth and a destruction of the things on the earth by fierce fire, which recurs at long intervals. At such times all they that dwell on the mountains and in high and dry places suffer destruction more than those who dwell near to rivers or the sea; and in our case the Nile, our Saviour in other ways, saves us also at such times from this calamity by rising high. And when, on the other hand, the Gods purge the earth with a flood of waters, all the herdsmen and shepherds that are in the mountains are saved, but those in the cities of your land are swept into the sea by the streams; whereas in our country neither then nor at any other time does the water pour down over our fields from above, on the contrary it all tends naturally to swell up from below. Hence it is, for these reasons, that what is here preserved is reckoned to be the most ancient; the truth being that in every place where there is no excessive heat or cold to prevent it there always exists some human stock, now more, now less in number. And if any event has occurred that is noble or great or in any way conspicuous, whether it be in your country or in ours or in some other place of which we know by report, all such events are recorded from of old and preserved here in our temples; whereas your people and the others are but newly equipped, every time, with letters and all such arts as civilised States require; and when, after the usual interval of years, like a plague, the flood from heaven comes sweeping down afresh upon your people, it leaves none of you but the unlettered and the uncultured, so that you become young as ever, with no knowledge of all that happened in old times in this land or in your own. Certainly the genealogies which you related just now, Solon, concerning the peoples of your country, are little better than children's tales; for, in the first place, you remember but one deluge, though many had occurred previously; and next, you are ignorant of the fact that the noblest and most perfect race amongst men were born in the land where you now dwell, and from them both you yourself are sprung and the whole of your existing city, out of some little seed that chanced to be left over; but this has escaped your notice because for many generations the survivors died with no power to express themselves in writing. For verily at one time, Solon, before the greatest destruction by water, what is now the Athenian state was the bravest in war and supremely well organised also in other respects. It is said that it possessed the most splendid works of art and the noblest polity of any nation under heaven of which we have heard tell.'

Upon hearing this, Solon said that he marvelled, and with the utmost eagerness requested the priest to recount for him in order and exactly all the facts about those citizens of old. The priest then said, 'I begrudge you not the story, Solon; nay, I will tell it, both for your own sake and that of your city, and most of all for the sake of the Goddess who has adopted for her own both your land and this of ours, and has nurtured and trained them – yours first by the space of a thousand years, when she had received the seed of you from Gê and Hephaestus, and after that ours. And the duration of our civilisation as set down in our sacred writings is 8,000 years. Of the citizens, then, who lived 9,000 years ago, I will declare to you briefly certain of their laws and the noblest of the deeds they performed: the full account in precise order and detail we shall go through later at our leisure, taking the actual writings. To get a view of their laws, look at the laws here; for you will find existing here at the present time many examples of the laws which then existed in your city. You see, first, how the priestly class is separated off from the rest; next, the class of craftsmen, of which each sort works by itself without mixing with any other; then the classes of shepherds, hunters and farmers, each distinct and separate. Moreover, the military class here, as no doubt you have noticed, is kept apart from all the other classes, being enjoined by the law to devote itself solely to the task of training for war. A further feature is the character of their equipment with shields and spears; for we were the first of the peoples of Asia to adopt these weapons, it being the Goddess who instructed us, even as she instructed you first of all the dwellers in yonder lands. Again, with regard to wisdom, you perceive, no doubt, the law here – how much attention it has devoted from the very beginning to the Cosmic Order, by discovering all the effects which the divine causes produce on human life, down to divination and the art of medicine which aims at health, and by its mastery also of all the subsidiary studies. So when, at that time, the Goddess had furnished you, before all others, with all this orderly and regular system, she established your State, choosing the spot wherein you were born since she perceived therein a climate duly blended, and how that it would bring forth men most like unto herself, and this first she established. Wherefore you lived under the rule of such laws as these – yea, and laws still better – and you surpassed all men in every virtue, as became those who were the offspring and nurselings of gods. Many, in truth, and great are the achievements of your State, which are a marvel to men as they are here recorded; but there is one which stands out above all both for magnitude and for nobleness. For it is related in our records how once upon a time your State stayed the course of a mighty host, which, starting from a distant point in the Atlantic Ocean, was insolently advancing to attack the whole of Europe, and Asia to boot. For the ocean there was at that time navigable; for in front of the mouth which you Greeks call, as you say, 'the pillars of Heracles', there lay an island which was larger than Libya and Asia together; and it was possible for the travellers of that time to cross from it to the other islands, and from the islands to the whole of the continent over against them which encompasses that veritable ocean. For all that we have here, lying within the mouth of which we speak, is evidently a haven having a narrow entrance; but that yonder is a real ocean, and the land surrounding it may most rightly be called, in the fullest and truest sense, a continent. Now in this island of Atlantis, there existed a confederation of kings, of great and marvellous power, which held sway over all the island, and over many other islands also and parts of the continent; and, moreover, of the lands here within the Straits they ruled over Libya as far as Egypt, and over Europe as far as Tuscany. So this host, being all gathered together, made an attempt one time to enslave by one single onslaught both your country and ours and the whole of the territory within the Straits. And then it was, Solon, that the manhood of your State showed itself conspicuous for valour and might in the sight of the world. For it stood pre-eminent above all in gallantry and all warlike arts, and acting partly as leader of the Greeks, and partly standing alone by itself when deserted by all others, and after encountering the deadliest perils, it defeated the invaders and reared a trophy; whereby it saved from slavery such as were not yet enslaved, and all the rest of us who dwell within the bounds of Heracles it ungrudgingly set free. But at a later time there occurred portentous earthquakes and floods, and one grievous day and night befell them, when the whole body of your warriors was swallowed up by the earth, and the island of Atlantis in like manner was swallowed up by the sea and vanished; wherefore also the ocean at that spot has now become impassable and unsearchable, being blocked up by the shoal mud which the island created as it settled down.

Critias 108E–121C

The tale is continued when after describing the merits of the ancient state of Athens, the speaker proceeds to give an account of their adversary, the island of Atlantis.

YOU, my dear Hermocrates, are posted in the last rank, with another man before you, so you are still courageous. But experience of your task will of itself speedily enlighten you as to its character. However, I must trust to your consolation and encouragement, and in addition to the gods you mentioned I must call upon all the rest and especially upon Mnemosyne. For practically all the most important part of our speech depends upon this goddess; for if I can sufficiently remember and report the tale once told by the priests and brought hither by Solon, I am well nigh convinced that I shall appear to the present audience to have fulfilled my task adequately. This, then, I must at once proceed to do, and procrastinate no longer.

Now first of all we must recall the fact that 9,000 is the sum of years since the war occurred, as is recorded, between the dwellers beyond the pillars of Heracles and all that dwelt within them; which war we have now to relate in detail. It was stated that this city of ours was in command of the one side and fought through the whole of the war, and in command of the other side were the kings of the island of Atlantis, which we said was an island larger than Libya and Asia once upon a time, but now lies sunk by earthquakes and has created a barrier of impassable mud which prevents those who are sailing out from here from proceeding further. Now as regards the numerous barbaric tribes and all the Hellenic nations that then existed, the sequel of our story, when it is, as it were, unrolled, will disclose what happened in each locality; but the facts about the Athenians of that age and the enemies with whom they fought we must necessarily describe first, at the outset – the military power, that is to say, of each and their forms of government. And of these two we must give the priority in our account to the State of Athens.

Once upon a time the gods were taking over by lot the whole earth according to its regions – not according to the results of strife; for it would not be reasonable to suppose that the gods were ignorant of their own several rights, nor yet that they attempted to obtain for themselves by means of strife a possession to which others, as they knew, has a better claim. So by just allotments they received each one his own, and they settled their countries, and when they had thus settled them, they reared us up, even as herdsmen rear their flocks, to be their cattle and their nurselings; only it was not our bodies that they constrained by bodily force, like shepherds guiding their flocks by stroke of staff, but they directed from the stern where the living creature is easiest to turn about, laying hold on the soul by persuasion, as by a rudder, according to their own disposition; and thus they drove and steered all the mortal kind. Now in other regions others of the gods had their allotments and ordered the affairs, but inasmuch as Hephaestus and Athena were of a like nature, being born of the same father, and agreeing, moreover, in their love of wisdom and craftsmanship, they both took for their joint portion this land of ours as being naturally congenial and adapted for virtue and wisdom, and therein they planted as native to the soil men of virtue and ordained to their mind the mode of government. And of these citizens the names are preserved, but their works have vanished owing to the repeated destruction of their successors and the length of the intervening periods. For, as we said before, the stock that survived on each occasion was a remnant of unlettered mountaineers which had heard the names only of the rulers, and but little besides of their works. So though they gladly passed on these names to their descendants, concerning the mighty deeds and the laws of their predecessors they had no knowledge, save for some invariably obscure reports; and since, moreover, they and their children for many generations were in want of the necessaries of life, their attention was given to their own needs and all their talk was about them; and in consequence they paid no regard to the happenings of bygone ages. For legendary lore and the investigation of antiquity are visitants that come to cities in company with leisure, when they see that men are already furnished with the necessaries of life, and not before.

In this way, then, the names of the ancients, without their works, have been preserved. And for evidence of what I say I point to the statement of Solon, that the Egyptian priests, in describing the war of that period, mentioned most of those names – such as those of Cecrops and Erechtheus and Erichthonius and Erysichthon and most of the other names which are recorded of the various heroes before Theseus – and in like manner also the names of the women. Moreover, the habit and figure of the goddess indicate that in the case of all animals, male and female, that herd together, every species is naturally capable of practising as a whole and in common its own proper excellence.

Now at that time there dwelt in this country not only the other classes of the citizens who are occupied in the handicrafts and in the raising of food from the soil, but also the military class, which had been separated off at the commencement by divine heroes and dwelt apart. It was supplied with all that was required for its sustenance and training, and none of its members possessed any private property, but they regarded all they had as the common property of all; and from the rest of the citizens they claimed to receive nothing beyond a sufficiency of sustenance; and they practised all those pursuits which were mentioned yesterday, in the description of our proposed 'guardians'. Moreover, what was related about our country was plausible and true, namely, that, in the first place, it had its boundaries at that time marked off by the Isthmus, and on the inland side reaching to the heights of Cithaeron and Parnes; and that the boundaries ran down with Cropia on the right, and on the seaward side they shut off the Asopus on the left; and that all other lands were surpassed by ours in the goodness of soil, so that it was actually able at that period to support a large host which was exempt from the labours of husbandry. And of its goodness a strong proof is this: what is now left of our soil rivals any other in being all productive and abundant in crops and rich in pasturage for all kinds of cattle; and at that period, in addition to their fine quality it produced these things in vast quantity. How, then, is this statement plausible, and what residue of the land then existing serves to confirm its truth? The whole of the land lies like a promontory jutting out from the rest of the continent far into the sea; and all the cup of the sea round about it is, as it happens, of a great depth. Consequently, since many great convulsions took place during the 9,000 years – for such was the number of years from that time to this – the soil which has kept breaking away from the highlands during these ages and these disasters, forms no pile of sediment worth mentioning, as in other regions, but keeps sliding away ceaselessly and disappearing in the deep. And, just as happens in small islands, what now remains compared to what then existed is like the skeleton of a sick man, all the fat and soft earth having wasted away, and only the bare framework of the land being left. But at that epoch the country was unimpaired, and for its mountains it had high arable hills, and in place of the 'moorlands' as they are now called, it contained plains full of rich soil; and it had much forest-land in its mountains, of which there are visible signs even to this day; for there are some mountains which now have nothing but food for bees, but they had trees no very long time ago, and the rafters from those felled there to roof the largest building are still sound. And besides, there were many lofty trees of cultivated species; and it produced boundless pasturage for flocks. Moreover, it was enriched by the yearly rains from Zeus, which were not lost to it, as now, by flowing from the bare land into the sea; but the soil it had was deep, and therein it received the water, storing it up in the retentive loamy soil; and by drawing off into the hollows from the heights the water that was there absorbed, it provided all the various districts with abundant supplies of spring-waters and streams, whereof the shrines which still remain even now, at the spots where the fountains formerly existed, are signs which testify that our present description of the land is true.

Such, then, was the natural condition of the rest of the country, and it was ornamented as you would expect from genuine husbandmen who made husbandry their sole task, and who were also men of taste and of native talent, and possessed of most excellent land and a great abundance of water, and also, above the land, a climate of most happily tempered seasons. And as to the city, this is the way in which it was laid out at that time. In the first place, the Acropolis, as it existed then, was different from what it is now. For as it is now, the action of a single night of extraordinary rain has crumbled it away and made it bare of soil, when earthquakes occurred simultaneously with the third of the disastrous floods which preceded the destructive deluge in the time of Deucalion. But in its former extent, at an earlier period, it went down towards the Eridanus and the Ilissus, and embraced within it the Pnyx; and it was all rich in soil and, save for a small space, level on the top. And its outer parts, under its slopes, were inhabited by the craftsmen and such of the husbandmen as had their farms close by; but on the topmost part only the military class by itself had its dwelling round about the temple of Athene and Hephaestus, surrounding themselves with a single ring-fence, which formed, as it were, the enclosure of a single dwelling. On the northward side of it they had established their public dwellings and winter mess rooms, and all the arrangements in the way of buildings which were required for the community life of themselves and the priests, but all was devoid of gold or silver, of which they made no use anywhere; on the contrary, they aimed at a mean between luxurious display and meanness, and built themselves tasteful houses, wherein they and their children's children grew old and handed them on in succession unaltered to others like themselves. As for the southward parts, when they vacated their gardens and gymnasia and messrooms as was natural in the summer, they used them for these purposes. And near the place of the present Acropolis there was one spring – which was choked up by the earthquakes so that but small tricklings of it are now left round about; but to the men of that time it afforded a plentiful stream for them all, being well tempered both for winter and summer. In this fashion, then, they dwelt, acting as guardians of their own citizens and as leaders, by their own consent, of the rest of the Greeks; and they watched carefully that their own numbers, of both men and women, who were neither too young nor too old to fight, should remain for all times as nearly as possible the same, namely, about 20,000.

So it was that these men, being themselves of the character described and always justly administering in some such fashion both their own land and Hellas, were famous throughout all Europe and Asia both for their bodily beauty and for the perfection of their moral excellence, and were of all men then living the most renowned. And now, if we have not lost recollection of what we heard when we were still children, we will frankly impart to you all, as friends, our story of the men who warred against our Athenians, what their state was and how it originally came about.

But before I begin my account, there is still a small point which I ought to explain, lest you should be surprised at frequently hearing Greek names given to barbarians. The reason of this you shall now learn. Since Solon was planning to make use of the story for his own poetry, he had found, on investigating the meaning of the names, that those Egyptians who had first written them down had translated them into their own tongue. So he himself in turn recovered the original sense of each name and, rendering it into our tongue, wrote it down so. And these very writings were in the possession of my grandfather and are actually now in mine, and when I was a child I learnt them all by heart. Therefore if the names you hear are just like our local names, do not be at all astonished; for now you know the reason for them. The story then told was a long one, and it began something like this.

Like as we previously stated concerning the allotments of the gods, that they portioned out the whole earth, here into larger allotments and there into smaller, and provided for themselves shrines and sacrifices, even so Poseidon took for his allotment the island of Atlantis and settled therein the children whom he had begotten of a mortal woman in a region of the island of the following description.

Bordering on the sea and extending through the centre of the whole island there was a plain, which is said to have been the fairest of all plains and highly fertile; and, moreover, near the plain, at a distance of about 50 stades, there stood a mountain that was low on all sides. Thereon dwelt one of the natives originally sprung from the earth, Evenor by name, with his wife Leucippe; and they had for offspring an only-begotten daughter, Cleito. And when this damsel was now come to marriageable age, her mother died and also her father; and Poseidon, being smitten with desire for her, wedded her; and to make the hill whereon she dwelt impregnable he broke it off all round about; and he made circular belts of sea

The dwelling of Poseidon.

and land enclosing one another alternately, some greater, some smaller, two being of land and three of sea, which he carved as it were out of the midst of the island; and these belts were at even distances on all sides, so as to be impassable for man; for at that time neither ships nor sailing were as yet in existence. And Poseidon himself set in order with ease, as a god would, the central island, bringing up from beneath the earth two springs of waters, the one flowing warn from its source, the other cold, and producing out of the earth all kinds of food in plenty. And he begat five pairs of twin sons and reared them up; and when he had divided all the island of Atlantis into ten portions, he assigned to the first-born of the eldest sons his mother's dwelling and the allotment surrounding it, which was the largest and the best; and him he appointed to be king over the rest, and the others to be rulers, granting to each the rule over many men and a large tract of country. And to all of them he gave names, giving to him that was eldest and king the name after which the whole island was called and the sea spoken of as the Atlantic, because the first king who then reigned had the name of Atlas. And the name of his younger twin-brother, who had for his portion the extremity of the island near the pillars of Heracles up to the part of the country now called Gadeira after the name of that region, was Eumelus in Greek, but in the native tongue Gadeirus – which fact may have given its title to the country. And of the pair that were born next he called the one Ampheres and the other Evaemon; and of the third pair the older was named Mneseus and the younger Autochthon; and of the fourth pair, he called the first Elasippus and the second Mestor; and of the fifth pair, Azaes was the name given to the elder, and Diaprepes to the second. So all these, themselves and their descendants, dwelt for many generations bearing rule over many other islands throughout the sea, and holding sway besides, as was previously stated, over the Mediterranean peoples as far as Egypt and Tuscany.

Now a large family of distinguished sons sprang from Atlas; but it was the eldest, who, as king, always passed on the sceptre to the eldest of his sons, and thus they preserved the sovereignty for many generations; and the wealth they possessed was so immense that the like had never been seen before in any royal house nor will ever easily be seen again; and they were provided with everything of which provision was needed either in the city or throughout the rest of the country. For because of their headship they had a large supply of imports from abroad, and the island itself furnished most of the requirements of daily life – metals, to begin with, both the hard kind and the fusible kind, which are extracted by mining, and also that kind which is now known only by name but was more than a name then, there being mines of it in many places of the island – I mean 'orichalcum', which was the most precious of the metals then known, except gold. It brought forth also in abundance all the timbers that a forest provides for the labours of carpenters; and of animals it produced a sufficiency, both of tame and of wild. Moreover it contained a very large stock of elephants; for there was an ample food supply not only for all the other animals which haunt the marshes and lakes and rivers, or the mountains or the plains, but likewise also for this animal, which of its nature is the largest and most voracious. And in addition to all this, it produced and brought to perfection all those sweet-scented stuffs which the earth produces now, whether made of roots or herbs or trees, or of liquid gums derived from flowers or fruits. The cultivated fruit also, and the dry, which serves us for nutriment, and all the other kinds that we use for our meals – the various species of which are comprehended under the name 'vegetables' – and all the produce of trees which affords liquid and solid food and unguents, and the fruit of the orchard trees, so hard to store, which is grown for the sake of amusement and pleasure, and all the after-dinner fruits that we serve up as welcome remedies for the sufferer from repletion – all these that hallowed island, as it lay then beneath the sun, produced in marvellous beauty and endless abundance. And thus, receiving from the earth all these products, they furnished forth their temples and royal dwellings, their harbours and their docks, and all the rest of their country, ordering all in the fashion following.

First of all they bridged over the circles of sea which surrounded the ancient metropolis, making thereby a road towards and from the royal palace. And they had built the palace at the very beginning where the settlement was first made by their God and their ancestors; and as each king received it from his predecessor, he added to its adornment and did all he could to surpass the king before him, until finally they made of it an abode amazing to behold for the magnitude and beauty of its workmanship. For, beginning at the sea, they bored a channel right through to the outermost circle, which was three plethra in breadth, one hundred feet in depth, and fifty stades in length; and thus they made the entrance to it from the sea like that to a harbour by opening out a mouth large enough for the largest ships to sail through. Moreover, through the circles of land, which divided those of sea, over against the bridges they opened out a channel leading from circle to circle, large enough to give passage to a single trireme; and this they roofed over so that the sea-way was subterranean; for the lips of the land-circles were raised a sufficient height above the level of the sea. The greatest of the circles into which a boring was made for the sea was three stades in breadth, and the circle of land next to it was of equal breadth; and of the second pair of circles that of water was two stades in breadth and that of dry land equal again to the preceding one of water; and the circle which ran round the central island itself was of a stade's breadth. And this island, wherein stood the royal palace, was of five stades in diameter. Now the island and the circles and the bridge, which was a plethrum in breadth, they encompassed round about, on this side and on that, with a wall of stone; and upon the bridges on each side, over against the passages for the sea, they erected towers and gates. And the stone they quarried beneath the central island all round, and from beneath the outer and inner circles, some of it being white, some black and some red; and while quarrying it they constructed two inner docks, hollowed out and roofed over by the native rock. And of the buildings some they framed of one simple colour, in others they wove a pattern of many colours by blending the stones for the sake of ornament so as to confer upon the buildings a natural charm. And they covered with brass, as though with a plaster, all the circumference of the wall which surrounded the outermost circle; and that of the inner one they coated with tin; and that which encompassed the acropolis itself with orichalcum which sparkled like fire.

The royal palace within the acropolis was arranged in this manner. In the centre there stood a temple sacred to Cleito and Poseidon, which was reserved as holy ground, and encircled with a wall of gold; this being the very spot where at the beginning they had generated and brought to birth the family of the ten royal lines. Thither also they brought year by year from all the ten allotments their seasonable offerings to do sacrifice to each of those princes. And the temple of Poseidon himself was a stade in length, three plethra in breadth, and of a height which appeared symmetrical therewith; and there was something of the barbaric in its appearance. All the exterior of the temple they coated with silver, save only the pinnacles, and these they coated with gold. As to the interior, they made the roof all of ivory in appearance, variegated with gold and silver and orichalcum, and all the rest of the walls and pillars and floors they covered with orichalcum. And they placed therein golden statues, one being that of the God standing on a chariot and driving six winged steeds, his own figure so tall as to touch the ridge of the roof, and round about him a hundred Nereids on dolphins (for that was the number of them as men then believed); and it contained also many other images, the votive offerings of private men. And outside, round about the temple, there stood images in gold of all the princes, both themselves and their wives, as many as were descended from the ten kings, together with many other votive offerings both of the kings and of private persons not only from the State itself but also from all the foreign peoples over whom they ruled. And the altar, in respect of its size and its work-

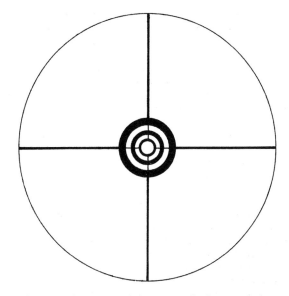

The Royal Metropolis, origin of the Cross of Atlantis. South American cities were similarly divided into four quarters.

manship, harmonised with its surroundings; and the royal palace likewise was such as befitted the greatness of the kingdom, and equally befitted the splendour of the temples.

The springs they made use of, one kind being of cold, another of warm water, were of abundant volume, and each kind was wonderfully well adapted for use because of the natural taste and excellence of its waters; and these they surrounded with buildings and with plantations of trees such as suited the waters; and, moreover, they set reservoirs round about, some under the open sky, and others under cover to supply hot baths in the winter; they put separate baths for the kings and for the private citizens, besides others for women, and others again for horses and all other beasts of burden, fitting out each in an appropriate manner. And the outflowing water they conducted to the sacred grove of Poseidon, which contained trees of all kinds that were of marvellous beauty and height because of the richness of the soil; and by means of channels they led the water to the outer circles over against the bridges. And there they had constructed many temples for gods, and many gardens and exercising grounds, some for men and some set apart for horses, in each of the circular belts of island; and besides the rest they had in the centre of the large island a racecourse laid out for horses, which was a stade in width, while as to length, a strip which ran round the whole circumference was reserved for equestrian contests. And round about it, on this side, and on that, were barracks for the greater part of the spearmen; but the guard-house of the more trusty of them was posted in the smaller circle, which was nearer the acropolis; while those who were the most trustworthy of all had dwellings granted to them within the acropolis round about the persons of the kings.

And the shipyards were full of triremes and all the tackling that belongs to triremes, and they were all amply equipped.

Such then was the state of things round about the abode of the kings. And after crossing the three outer harbours, one found a wall which began at the sea and ran round in a circle, at a uniform distance of fifty stades from the largest circle and harbour, and its ends converged at the seaward end of the channel. The whole of this wall had numerous houses built on to it, set close together; while the sea-way and the largest harbour were filled with ships and merchants coming from all quarters, which by reason of their multitude caused clamour and tumult of every description and an unceasing din night and day.

Now as regards the city and the environs of the ancient dwelling we have now well nigh completed the description as it was originally given. We must endeavour next to repeat the account of the rest of the country, what its natural character was, and in what fashion it was ordered. In the first place, then, according to the account, the whole region rose sheer out of the sea to a great height, but the part about the city was all a smooth plain, enclosing it round about, and being itself encircled by mountains which stretched as far as to the sea; and this plain had a level surface and was as a whole rectangular in shape, being 3,000 stades long on either side and 2,000 stades wide at its centre, reckoning upwards from the sea. And this region, all along the island, faced towards the South and was sheltered from the Northern blasts. And the mountains which surrounded it were at that time celebrated as surpassing all that now exist in number, magnitude and beauty; for they had upon them many rich villages of country folk, and streams and lakes and meadows which furnished ample nutriment to all the animals both tame and wild, and timber of various sizes and descriptions, abundantly sufficient for the needs of all and every craft.

Now as a result of natural forces, together with the labours of many kings which extended over many ages, the condition of the plain was this. It was originally a quadrangle, rectilinear for the most part, and elongated; and what it lacked of this shape they made right by means of a trench dug round about it. Now, as regards the depth of this trench and its breadth and length, it seems incredible that it should be so large as the account states, considering that it was made by hand, and in addition to all the other operations, but none the less we must report what we heard; it was dug out to the depth of a plethrum and to a uniform breadth of a stade, and since it was dug round the whole of the plain its consequent length was 10,000 stades. It received the streams which came down from the mountains and after circling round the plain, and coming towards the city on this side and on that, it discharged them thereabouts in to the sea. And on the inland side of the city channels were cut in straight lines, of about 100 feet in width, across the plain, and these discharged themselves into the trench on the seaward side, the distance between each being 100 stades. It was in this way that they conveyed to the city the timber from the mountains and transported also on boats the seasons' products, by cutting transverse passages from one channel to the next and also to the city. And they cropped the land twice a year, making use of the rains from Heaven in the winter, and the waters that issue from the earth in summer, by conducting the streams from the trenches.

As regards their man-power, it was ordained that each allotment should furnish one man as leader of all the men in the plain who were fit to bear arms; and the size of the allotment was about ten times ten stades, and the total number of all the allotments was 60,000; and the number of the men in the mountains and in the rest of the country was countless, according to the report, and according to their districts and villages they were all assigned to these allotments under their leaders. So it was ordained that each such leader should provide for war the sixth part of a war-chariot's equipment, so as to make up 10,000 chariots in all, together with two horses and mounted men; also a pair of horses without a car, and attached thereto a combatant with a small shield and for charioteer the rider who springs from horse to horse; and two hoplites; and archers and slingers, two of each; and light-armed slingers and javelin-men, three of each; and four sailors towards the manning of twelve hundred ships. Such then were the military dispositions of the royal City; and those of the other nine varied in various ways, which it would take a long time to tell.

Of the magistracies and posts of honour the disposition, ever since the beginning, was this. Each of the ten kings ruled over the

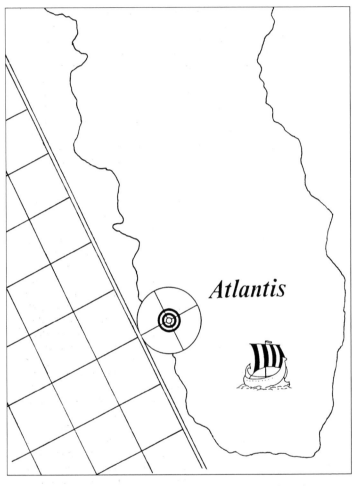

The perimeter canal approached the city on both sides where it
discharged into the sea, according to Lee, through the canal running
through the city.

men and most of the laws in his own particular portion and throughout his own city, punishing and putting to death whomsoever he
willed. But their authority over one another and their mutual rela-
tions were governed by the precepts of Poseidon, as handed down
to them by the law and by the records inscribed by the first princes
on a pillar of orichalcum, which was placed within the temple of
Poseidon in the centre of the island; and thither they assembled
every fifth year, and then alternately every sixth year – giving equal
honour to both the even and the odd – and when thus assembled
they took counsel about public affairs and inquired if any had in
any way transgressed and gave judgement. And when they were
about to give judgement they first gave pledges one to another of
the following description. In the sacred precincts of Poseidon there
were bulls at large; and the ten princes, being alone by themselves,
after praying to the God that they might capture a victim well-
pleasing unto him, hunted after the bulls with staves and nooses
but with no weapons of iron; and whatsoever bull they captured
they led up to the pillar and cut its throat over the top of the pillar,
raining down blood on the inscription. And inscribed upon the
pillar, besides the laws, was an oath which invoked mighty curses
upon them that disobeyed. When then, they had done sacrifice
according to their laws and were consecrating all the limbs of the
bull, they mixed a bowl of wine and poured in on behalf of each
one a gout of blood, and the rest they carried to the fire, when they
had first purged the pillars round about. And after this they drew
out from the bowl with golden ladles, and making libation over the
fire swore to give judgement according to the laws upon the pillar
and to punish whosoever had committed any previous transgression; and, moreover, that henceforth they would not transgress
any of the writings willingly, nor govern nor submit to any govern-
or's edict save in accordance with their father's laws. And when each
of them had made this invocation both for himself and for his seed
after him, he drank of the cup and offered it up as a gift in the
temple of the God, and after spending the interval in supping and
necessary business, when darkness came on and the sacrificial fire
had died down, all the princes robed themselves in most beautiful
sable vestments, and sat on the ground beside the cinders of the
sacrificial victims throughout the night, extinguishing all the fire that
was round about the sanctuary; and there they gave and received
judgement, if any one of them accused any of committing any
transgression. And when they had given judgement, they wrote the
judgements, when it was light, upon a golden tablet, and dedicated
them together with their robes as memorials. And there were many

other special laws concerning the peculiar rights of the several princes, whereof the most important were these: that they should never take up arms against one another, and that, should anyone attempt to overthrow in any city their royal house, they should all lend aid, taking counsel in common, like their forerunners, concerning their policy in war and other matters, while conceding the leadership to the royal branch of Atlas; and that the king had no authority to put to death any of his brother-princes save with the consent of more than half of the ten.

Such then was the magnitude and character of the power which existed in those regions at that time; and this power the God set in array and brought against these regions of ours on some such pretext as the following, according to the story. For many generations, so long as the inherited nature of the God remained strong in them, they were submissive to the laws and kindly disposed to their divine kindred. For the intents of their hearts were true and in all ways noble, and they showed gentleness joined with wisdom in dealing with the changes and chances of life and in their dealings one with another. Consequently they thought scorn of everything save virtue and lightly esteemed their rich possessions, bearing with ease the burden, as it were, of the vast volume of their gold and other goods; thus their wealth did not make them drunk with pride so that they lost control of themselves and went to ruin; rather, in their soberness of mind they clearly saw that all these good things are increased by general amity combined with virtue, whereas the eager pursuit and worship of these goods not only causes the goods themselves to diminish but makes virtue also to perish with them. As a result, then, of such reasoning and of the continuance of their divine nature all their wealth had grown to such a greatness as we previously described. But when the portion of divinity within them was now becoming faint through being ofttimes blended with a large measure of mortality, whereas the human temper was becoming dominant, then at length they lost their comeliness, through being unable to bear the burden of their possessions, and became ugly to look upon, in the eyes of him who has the gift of sight; for they had lost the fairest of their goods from the most precious of their parts; but in the eyes of those who have no gift of perceiving what is the truly happy life, it was then above all that they appeared to be superlatively fair and blessed, filled as they were with lawless ambition and power. And Zeus, the God of gods, who reigns by law, inasmuch as he has the gift of perceiving such things, marked how this righteous race was in evil plight, and desired to inflict punishment upon them, to the end that when chastised they might

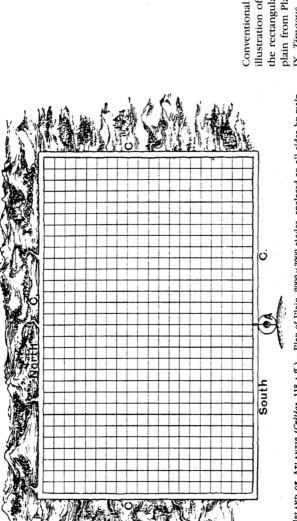

THE ISLAND OF ATLANTIS (*Critias*, 118 A ff.).—Plan of Plain, 2000×3000 stades, enclosed on all sides by main canal (C), 10,000 stades long, and intersected by 20 vertical and 19 horizontal cross-trenches. On all sides except the south the plain is encircled by mountains, with streams, villages, forests, etc. At its central point (A) on the south the canal is joined by the canal which runs through the city to the sea.

Frontispiece

Conventional illustration of the rectangular plain from Plato IX, *Timaeus*, *Critias* etc. (Harvard University Press) strike a truer note. Wherefore he assembled together all the gods into that abode which they honour most, standing as it does at the centre of all the Universe, and beholding all things that partake of generation; and when he had assembled them, he spake thus: . . .

CHAPTER 4

Donnelly's Account

IGNATIUS DONNELLY was for many years a Republican congressman in the USA until forced to retire due to pressure of party politics. He subsequently devoted most of his time to study in the Library of Congress and in 1882 published his monumental work *Atlantis: The Antediluvian World*.

It was this work more than any other which began the modern enthusiasm for the Atlantis legend and perpetuated the myth of Atlantis as a continent sunk in the Atlantic Ocean and in the first statement of the opening paragraph Donnelly sets out his primary objective to prove:

1. That there once existed in the Atlantic Ocean, opposite the mouth of the Mediterranean Sea, a large island, which was the remnant of an Atlantic continent, and known to the ancient world as Atlantis.

There then follows a table setting out the remaining twelve purposes of his scholarly work, to propose:

2. That the description of this island given by Plato is not, as has been long supposed, fable, but veritable history.

3. That Atlantis was the region where man first rose from a state of barbarism to civilisation.

4. That it became, in the course of ages, a populous and mighty nation, from whose overflowings the shores of the Gulf of Mexico, the Mississippi River, the Amazon, the Pacific coast of South America, the Mediterranean, the west coast of Europe and Africa, the Baltic, the Black Sea, and the Caspian were populated by civilised nations.

5. That it was the true Antediluvian world; the Garden of Eden, the Gardens of the Hesperides, the Elysian Fields; the Gardens of Alcinous; the Mesomphalos; the Olympos; the Asgard of the traditions

51

of the ancient nations; representing a universal memory of a great land, where early mankind dwelt for ages in peace and happiness.

6. That the gods and goddesses of the ancient Greeks, the Phoenicians, the Hindoos, and the Scandinavians were simply the kings, queens, and heroes of Atlantis; and the acts attributed to them in mythology are a confused recollection of real historical events.

7. That the mythology of Egypt and Peru represented the original religion of Atlantis, which was sun-worship.

8. That the oldest colony formed by the Atlanteans was probably in Egypt, whose civilisation was a reproduction of that of the Atlantic island.

9. That the implements of the 'Bronze Age' of Europe were derived from Atlantis. The Atlanteans were also the first manufacturers of iron.

10. That the Phoenician alphabet, parent of all the European alphabets, was derived from an Atlantis alphabet, which was also conveyed from Atlantis to the Mayas of Central America.

11. That Atlantis was the original seat of the Aryan or Indo-European family of nations, as well as of the Semitic peoples, and possibly also of the Turanian races.

12. That Atlantis perished in a terrible convulsion of nature, in which the whole island sank into the ocean, with nearly all its inhabitants.

13. That a few persons escaped in ships and on rafts, and carried to the nations east and west the tidings of the appalling catastrophe, which has survived to our own time in the Flood and Deluge legends of the different nations of the old and new worlds.

It seems strange that although Donnelly refers to the works of classical writers, he seems to have overlooked works appearing after the discovery of America that suggested that America itself might have been Atlantis.

Sir Francis Bacon writing in the seventeenth century is often credited with being the first to identify America as the site of Atlantis. His unfinished book *The New Atlantis* was published posthumously in 1627. The editor of the modern (1900) edition tells us however that the first to identify the newly-discovered continent of America as Atlantis was not Bacon, but Francisco

Lopez de Gomara in his *Istoria de las Indias* published in Saragossa in 1552 and translated into English in 1555.

Francis Bacon was however a prominent politician, literary figure and considered one of the greatest English philosophers. Writing about an imaginary island in the Pacific Ocean and looking back at the history of the 'Great Atlantis', it is worth reproducing some of his actual text, as follows:

> You shall understand that about three thousand years ago, or somewhat more, the Navigation of the world (specially for remote voyages) was greater than at this day . . . Whether it was, that the example of the Ark, that saved the remnant of men from the Universal Deluge, gave men confidence to adventure upon the waters; or what it was; but such is the Truth. The Phoenicians, and specially the Tyrians, had great fleets. So had the Carthaginians their colony, which is yet further West. Towards the east the shipping of Egypt, and of Palestine was likewise great. China also, and the great Atlantis, (that you call America) which have now but junks, and canoes, abounded then in tall ships.
>
> At the same time, and an Age after, or more, the inhabitants of the great Atlantis did flourish . . . Yet so much is true, that the said country of Atlantis, as well that of Peru then called Coya, and that of Mexico then called Tyrambel, were mighty and proud kingdoms, in arms, shipping, and riches: so mighty as at one time (or at least within the space of 10 years) they both made two great expeditions; they of Tyrambel through the Atlantic to the Mediterranean Sea; and they of Coya through the South Sea . . . But whether it were the ancient Athenians, that had the glory of the Repulse, and resistance of these forces, I can say nothing. But certain it is, there never came back, either ship, or man, from that voyage.
>
> But the Divine Revenge overtook not long after those proud enterprises. For within less than the space of one hundred years, the Great Atlantis was utterly lost and destroyed: not by a great earthquake, as your man saith (for that whole tract is little subject to earthquakes); but by a particular Deluge or Inundation. Those countries having, at that day, far greater rivers, and far higher mountains, to pour down waters, than any part of the Old World. But it is true, that the same inundation was not deep; not past forty feet in most places from the ground. So that, although it destroyed man and beast generally, yet some few wild inhabitants of the wood escaped. For as for men, although they had buildings in many places, higher than the depth of the water, yet that inundation,

though it were shallow, had a long continuance; whereby they of the Vale, that were not drowned, perished for want of food, and other things necessary.

So as marvel you not at the thin population of America, nor at the rudeness and ignorance of the people . . . and having in their mountain regions been used to clothe themselves with the skins of tigers, bears and great hairy goats, when after they came down into the valley, they found the intolerable heats which are there, and knowing no means of lighter apparel they were forced to begin the custom of going naked, which continueth at this day. Only they take great delight in the feathers of birds. So you see, by this main accident of Time, we lost our trafick with the Americas, with whom we had most commerce.[57]

As a former scholar of Trinity College, Cambridge, did Francis Bacon consult ancient and rare books? Since it is worth commenting that not only is America correctly identified as Atlantis but the end (of the people) is stressed as being the result of *inundation* even quoting the depth of water to a depth of 40 ft! The inundation was also of a long continuance, forcing the displacement of the people – a different picture to a continent sunk under the sea!

Ignatius Donnelly had at his fingertips all the relevant information to back up the idea that America might be Atlantis, but he never seems to have suspected this. Instead he refers to the Mississippi Delta, Mexico and Peru as being colonies of Atlantis, which indeed they may have been, but not the Atlantis of Donnelly's vision rigidly following the precepts of Plato as an island continent sunk in the Atlantic but rather an Atlantis civilisation which was already part of the American continent and had flourished at an earlier time. He never seems to have suspected this although he quotes writers other than Plato who had made reference to a large island in the Atlantic, such as Homer, Plutarch and others; Silenas who tells Midas there was another continent besides Europe, Asia and Africa, 'a country where gold and silver are so plentiful that they are esteemed no more than we esteem iron' and Diodorus Siculus, the historian who lived in the age of Julius Caesar and Augustus, who relates that the Phoenicians discovered,

> . . . a large island in the Atlantic Ocean, beyond the Pillars of Hercules, several days' sail from the coast of Africa. The soil was exceedingly fertile; the scenery was diversified by rivers, mountains

A breast ornament from a tomb at Monte Alban, former territory of the
Mixtecs. Made of an alloy of gold and copper, it represents a worked
example of *Orichalcum*.

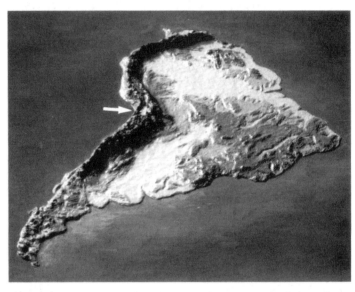

Model of the 'whole island' with the Altiplano arrowed. The translation from Plato by R. G. Bury reads 'bordering on the sea and extending through the centre of the whole island there was a plain.' The translation by Desmond Lee renders this as 'at the centre of the island, near the sea, was a plain' and adds the footnote: 'i.e. midway along its greatest length.'

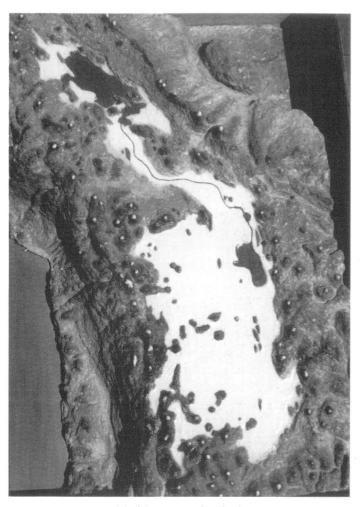

Model of the rectangular Altiplano.

The salt remains at Salar de Uyuni.

Volcanic caldera three miles in diameter, 50 stades from the centre of the plain and of great similarity to the mountain Plato described.

and forests; it was the custom of the inhabitants to retire during the summer to magnificent country-houses, which stood in the midst of beautiful gardens. Fish and game were found in great abundance; the climate was delicious, and the trees bore fruit at all seasons of the year.

Yet so much of the remainder of Donnelly's evidence seems to have been on the right lines, for example when he quotes the deluge legends of America . . . the *Popul Vuh* (sacred book) of the Central Americans:

Then the waters were agitated by the will of the Heart of Heaven (Hurakan), and a great inundation came upon the heads of these creatures . . . They were engulfed, and a resinous thickness descended from heaven; . . . the face of the earth was obscured, and a heavy darkening rain commenced – rain by day and rain by night . . . There was heard a great noise above their heads, as if produced by fire. Then were men seen running, pushing each other, filled with despair; they wished to climb upon their houses, and the houses, tumbling down, fell to the ground; they wished to climb upon the trees, and the trees shook them off; they wished to enter into the grottoes (caves), and the grottoes closed themselves before them . . . Water and fire contributed to the universal ruin at the time of the last great cataclysm which preceded the fourth creation.

And the Toltec legend of the flood:

It is found in the histories of the Toltecs [possible ancestors of the Aztecs] that this age and first world, as they called it, lasted 1716 years; that men were destroyed by tremendous rains and lightnings from the sky, and even all the land, without the exception of anything, and the highest mountains, were covered up and submerged in water fifteen cubits; and here they added other fables of how men came to multiply from the few who escaped in a 'toptli-petlocali'; that this word nearly signifies a closed chest; and how, after men had multiplied they erected a very high 'zacuali', which is today a tower of great height, in order to take refuge in it should the second world (age) be destroyed. Presently their languages were confused, and, not being able to understand each other, they went to different parts of the earth.

The Chaldean, Bible and American legends are compared, each

Eruption of volcano.

offering similarities such as: the depth of water that prevailed was fifteen cubits, the building of an ark, the sending out of a bird, the ark coming to rest on a mountain, the building of a high tower and subsequent confusion of languages – suggesting that America, or rather Atlantis as it should properly be called, was the site of the Garden of Eden.

Donnelly recognises the ancient works of Peru as pre-dating the Incas and has a certain admiration for the aqueducts of which the Peruvians made large use, one in particular being built of hewn stone and extending 450 miles over sierras and rivers, similarly the roads, built on masonry and extending the length of the empire.

> These roads were ancient in the time of the Incas. They were the work of the white, auburn haired, bearded men from Atlantis, thousands of years before the time of the Incas. When Huayna Capac marched his army over the main road to invade Quito, it was so old and decayed 'that he found great difficulties in the passage', and he immediately ordered the necessary reconstruction.

Of the wealth of Peru, Donnelly notes that gold and silver had no commercial value being reserved for the adornment of the temple walls as in Atlantis, further,

> their accumulations of the precious metals exceeded anything previously known in the history of the world. In the course of twenty-five years after the Conquest the Spaniards sent from Peru to Spain more then eight hundred million dollars of gold, nearly all of it taken from the Peruvians as 'booty'. In one of their palaces 'they had an artificial garden, the soil of which was made of pieces of fine gold, and this was artificially planted with different kinds of maize, which were of gold, their stems, leaves and ears. Besides this, they had more then twenty sheep [llamas] with their lambs, attended by shepherds, all made of gold.' In a description of one lot of golden articles sent to Spain in 1534 by Pizarro, there is mention of 'four llamas, ten statues of women of full size, and a cistern of gold, so curious that it excited the wonder of all'.

On the subject of bronze, Donnelly has a lot to say with the perceptive remarks that in Europe although the Bronze Age followed the Stone Age, the Bronze Age should have been preceded by a Copper Age where weapons were made of pure copper alone, before peoples learned how to mix in 10 per cent of tin to produce the alloy known as Bronze.

He suggests that it is only in the Americas, from Bolivia to Lake Superior that we find everywhere traces of a long-enduring Copper Age and that only along the shores of Lake Superior is there evidence of an industry related to pure copper and the manufacture of copper implements.

Yet copper needs the addition of tin for the production of the bronze alloy and it is in Bolivia that tin is most abundant in addition to the wealth of copper and other metals which exists there.

Bronze was therefore carried to and traded throughout Europe, Donnelly suggests, and this is demonstrated by common artefacts like bronze celts and bronze swords of similar design found in places as far apart as Switzerland, Ireland, Denmark and Africa and initially distributed by a sea-going people. The Phoenicians and Carthaginians were the heirs to this latter day sea-going trade but they themselves, according to Donnelly, were preceded by the Tokhari – a people taken prisoner in the great sea fight of Rameses III and the remnant of the great Atlantic race who developed the copper/bronze metals industry; whose name itself signifies the copper island or the copper mountains in the sea and source of the thousands of tons of copper and tin imported into Europe: *Atlantis.*

Poseidon, ruler of the seas.

CHAPTER 5

Atlantis, Crete and the Sea Peoples

THE SOLE AND original source of information on Atlantis lies in Plato's *Timaeus* and *Critias*. Plato emphasises that he is handing on the tale exactly as he heard it. The tale originated in the Delta town of Sais in Egypt, when a visiting Greek, Solon, was discussing history with the Egyptian priests. The Egyptians reproached him for attempting to relate the legend of Deucalion and the Flood saying that the Greeks were a young nation and knew nothing of ancient history. They then recounted to Solon the history of the periodic destructions of the earth and the history of Atlantis.

If we accept the history as it is given, then the age of Atlantis would be 11,500 years ago, at a time when Greece was a rich and prosperous country. Since then, the land had been gradually broken down and washed away until in Solon's time it was a mere skeleton compared to its original fatness.

The primary objection to such an early date is that there is no archaeological evidence of any such early civilisation in either Greece or Egypt so it is claimed that neither temples nor priests existed to record the legend. Egyptian civilisation is one of the world's oldest with the first dynasty beginning with the legendary King Menes who formed Upper and Lower Egypt into one kingdom in 3,100 BC.[36]

Prior to this, Lower Egypt (Egypt of the Delta) was a kingdom in its own right and its earliest settlements date back to possibly 5,000 BC. It had a capital at Sais and an affinity with Libya as well as Crete demonstrated by common objects such as the harpoon, figure of eight shield[37] (described by Homer but not believed until the 'throne room' at Knossos was uncovered by Arthur Evans with painted figure of eight shields on the walls) double axe etc. The goddess of Sais was Neith, as correctly outlined by Plato, and her emblem was the double shield.

The search for Atlantis naturally looks to the Atlantic, since Plato says it lay beyond the Pillars of Hercules (the Strait of Gibraltar) and how the mighty invading force started from a distant point in the Atlantic Ocean. The size of the island continent is likened to that of Libya and Asia combined and compared to the Atlantic Ocean the Mediterranean is seen as a sheltered haven or pond, a point about which Plato had some doubts since he says 'evidently' a haven.

Geological surveys prove that no continent the size of Atlantis has slid beneath the waves of the Atlantic Ocean and that a land mass of this size could not disappear in a single day and night. Here we must distinguish between the island continent of Atlantis and the island capital of Atlantis. The ancient metropolis, built around a volcanic dome, could easily have been overcome in a singe day and swallowed up by the sea which subsequently became choked with mud or volcanic ash.

In the centre of the island continent lay a rich and fertile plain, one of the finest in the world. The plain was of immense size, $3,000 \times 2,000$ stades and had a massive irrigation ditch running round it with lesser ditches across it. It was surrounded by lofty and beautiful mountains and the ditches across the plain served to transport crops and timber from the mountains to the royal city of Atlantis.

The legend tells us that the location of the city was formerly created by the god, Poseidon, as a dwelling place for himself and his mortal wife, Cleito. It was formed out of a low hill and had the configuration of central island five stades in diameter surrounded by alternate rings of land and water. It had been adapted and built up over many generations by the Atlanteans who built channels and bridges between the rings and a channel connecting the outermost ring of water to the sea, fifty stades distant.

Plato describes the city with the temple to Poseidon as being in the centre of the island, near the sea and on a plain surrounded by lofty mountains. The plain is itself evidently elevated since we are told 'the whole region rose sheer out of the sea to a great height' (Bury) or as translated by Lee, 'the region as a whole was said to be high above the level of the sea, from which it rose precipitously; the city was surrounded by a uniformly flat plain, which was in turn enclosed by mountains which came right down to the sea'. Yet the city lay only 50 stades from the sea and here we have a key to the whole mystery, since how could the city be inland, surrounded by mountains on an elevated plain yet only 50 stades (five Greek miles) from the sea? It would be impossible for oarsmen to row uphill to an elevated plain 'at a great height' over such a short distance as 50 stades unless of course the description applied to an *inland sea*. The trenches which drained it in winter would then serve to irrigate it in summer with the inland sea providing an excellent reservoir.

It is this description which enables us to precisely identify the location of Atlantis, since the Altiplano conforms exactly in every detail, being elevated, rectangular in shape i.e. 'rectilinear for the most part and elongated' . . . 'encircled by mountains which stretched as far as the sea' – meaning the Pacific yet with its own inland sea namely Lake Poopo; the whole region lies at the centre of the 'island' 'midway along its greatest length' (Lee), is at the same time 'next to the sea' (the Pacific) and the whole continent lies 'in front of the Pillars of Hercules'.

Although all the story is attributed to Solon, it is presented in such a way that in *Timaeus* it is related by an Egyptian priest and later, in *Critias*, the tale is resumed by a Greek where the introduction may reflect the *opinion* of Plato.

Thus the Egyptian priest says that Atlantis was 'swallowed up by the sea and vanished, so that the sea at that spot has now become impassable and unsearchable, being blocked up by the shoal mud which the island created as it settled down'. It is in *Critias* that Plato states, by way of a resumé, that the island sunk by earthquakes 'prevents those who are sailing out from here to the ocean beyond from proceeding further' thus implying, as he believed, that the sunken island lay immediately in front of the Strait of Gibraltar.

Again, the priest tells Solon that Athens was founded 9,000 years previously by the goddess Athena, and Egypt 1,000 years after that. It is in *Critias*, that 'we must recall the fact that 9,000 is the sum of years since the war occurred' and it should be noted that the same date, 9,000 years before Solon, is given both to the founding of Athens and the defeat and destruction of Atlantis.

Now the whole object of the priest's dissertation was to impress on Solon the antiquity of mankind and the comparative youthfulness of the Greek nation of which Solon was a member (around 590 BC). It is thus that he tells of the founding of Athens many years beforehand and how afterwards civilisations had risen and fallen and the landscape itself been altered by time. The people of Athens had been an exemplary race who maintained a standing army of 20,000 'guardians' renowned for their physical excellence and beauty, and as if to tell of their supreme achievement, the priest tells how '*once up a time*' they defeated the numerically superior enemy alliance and thus saved the free peoples of Greece, Egypt and the eastern Mediterranean from enslavement.

It was the priest's intention, after relating the history of Athens and 'the noblest deeds they performed', to go through later, at their leisure 'the full account in precise order and detail'. It seems odd then, that the date of this war was concurrent with the founding of Athens, since how could Atlantis enslave a country – Egypt – which according to the story was also not yet founded for another 1,000 years? Note also that we are told 'the kings and their descendants dwelt for many generations', so it is certain that the end of Atlantis occurred at a later period.

At the time of the war, Atlantis already ruled many islands and part of the 'continent', as well as Libya as far as Egypt and Europe as far as Tuscany. It therefore controlled most of the Mediterranean. In order to subdue the remaining peoples, Atlantis was preparing to deploy a huge military and naval force. Since the bulk of this force was to come overseas from Atlantis, they would have had to build up their army somewhere in the Mediterranean before launching their offensive. They already controlled the island of Sicily, and in the east of their empire lay the most strategic island in the eastern Mediterranean, an island between Greece and Egypt, described by Diodorus Siculus, a Greek historian living in Sicily in the 1st century BC, as 'especially well situated for expeditions against any part of the inhabited world'.

It seems reasonable to associate Crete with the empire of Atlantis since not only did the Minoans possess a powerful sea-going fleet, but they also indulged in the cult of the bull.

In Atlantis, the kings assembled and swore to uphold the sacred laws. This they did in a ceremony in which they captured a bull, led the animal up to a pillar on which the laws were inscribed and cut the bull's throat, bathing the inscription in blood. They then mixed blood with wine and drank to solemnise the oath. On Crete we find subterranean crypts, the dominant feature of which is a massive stone pillar, sometimes carved with the symbol of the double axe. The chambers also contain drains . . . presumably to take away the excess blood.

Crete, although perhaps one of the frontiers of the Atlantean empire, should never have been mistaken for the island of Atlantis itself as has been suggested by one modern theory. To begin with, it becomes necessary to remove the city metropolis from the plain, so that the metropolis is placed on Santorini and the plain remains on Crete. The islands of Santorini or Thera, lie 75 miles north of Crete and were originally one single volcanic island which was destroyed in a massive eruption around 1500 BC. This date is 900 years before Solon and assumes that a mistake has been made translating units of thousands into Greek, requiring a division by ten to correct it.

The plain of 3,000 × 2,000 stades is likewise divided by 10 to become 300 × 200 stades, small enough to supposedly fit onto the island of Crete, so that the Minoan civilisation could be said to have disappeared as a result of the Thera explosion. One objection to this theory is that Thera exploded in 1500 BC, but Minoan Crete was not overwhelmed until 100 years later, in 1400 BC.[21]

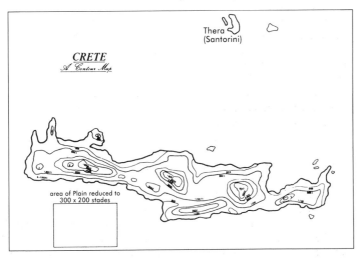

The island of Crete: a contour map.

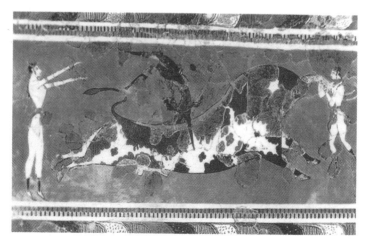

Bull-vaulting fresco from Crete.

In any case, even at the reduced size of 300 × 200 stades (30 × 20 nautical miles or 53 × 37 kms) the plain is still too large for Crete. It is not acceptable to separate the city from the plain in this manner since Plato clearly tells us 'the part about the city was all a smooth plain, enclosing it round about and being itself encircled by mountains which stretched as far as to the sea'. No rectangular plain encircled by mountains exists on Crete and no massive irrigation canals 600 ft wide have been found on Crete.

The island (city) of Atlantis was 'swallowed up by the sea and *vanished*' while Santorini clearly remains; one can even sail into its centre which is plainly not 'blocked up by the shoal mud which the island created as it settled down'.

Further, it is quite obvious that Crete is not outside the Pillars of Hercules, it is not a continent comparable in size to Libya and Asia together, neither has it ever contained elephants nor the abundance of metals such as gold, silver or tin, and it would of course be a nonsense, as has been suggested, to say that tin would be imported in sufficient quantities for the purpose of plating a city wall.

The civilisation of Minoan Crete was overwhelmed in 1400 BC,[21] when the palaces were burned and shortly afterwards destroyed by earthquakes. Could there have been an attacking force such as Plato described? A party of Athenians who 'after encountering the deadliest perils, defeated the invaders and reared a trophy'.

One possible outpost of the Atlantean empire was the city of Troy, which may have had links with Crete[39] and was made famous through Homer's account of the siege and fall of Troy which took place in 1260 BC.[20] One notable feature of this episode was the fleet of ships, numbering 1200, which sailed against Troy. This is the same number Plato gives for the fleet of Atlantis suggesting that either Plato had drawn on Homer's account to embellish his own, or that he had acquired another version of events from broadly the same period of history.

With the conquest of Crete, the Greeks entered their Golden Age, which lasted for two hundred years until they were invaded and occupied by the Dorians, the 'returning Heraclids': only Athens remained impregnable.[20]

The invaders swept down through Turkey towards Egypt and in 1220 BC the 'Sea Peoples' launched an invasion of Egypt simultaneously by land and by sea with a huge army entering Egypt from the Libyan desert.[23]

The Egyptian records tell us that the largest contingent was the Ekwesh, 'of the countries of the sea' . . . 'they were advancing on Egypt while the flame was prepared before them. Their league was Peleset, Tjeker, Shekelesh, Denyen and Weshesh, united lands. They laid their hands upon the lands to the very circuit of the Earth, their hearts confident and trusting "our plans will succeed".'

The Egyptians, like the Greeks, had oared galleys but the invaders, it would seem, had only sailing ships without oars.[30] Becalmed in the confines of the Delta, the invaders were outmanœuvered; grappling hooks were thrown into their rigging and the ships pulled over. This attack was beaten off and the slaughtered were numbered in thousands. Thousands more were led off into captivity later to be absorbed into the Egyptian nation or resettled, as in the case of the Philistines, along a narrow strip of land bordering the Mediterranean to the east of Egypt.

In 1186 BC another invasion took place and this time they were defeated by Rameses III, who 'trampled down the foreign countries, the isles who sailed over against his boundaries . . . the Peleset and Tursha coming from the midst of the sea'. But curiously, in

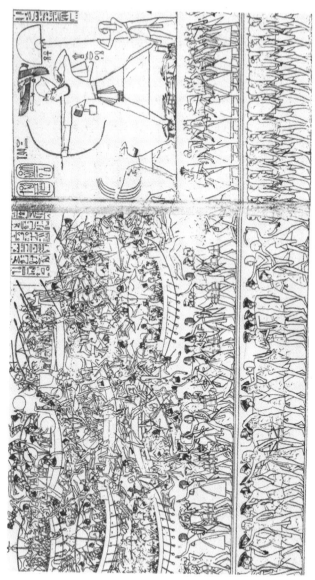

The great sea battle; the Sea Peoples are defeated by Rameses III and led off into captivity.

Philistine prisoners among the invading Sea Peoples captured by
Rameses III. Note the feathered head-dresses.

the second invasion the names of two major groups of attackers,
the Ekwesh and Lukka, are missing from the roll call.[23]

The similarity of this invasion by 'confederated nations', entering
from Libya etc and the description by Plato of a confederation
of kings ruling over Libya as far as Egypt and Europe as far as
Tuscany, attempting to enslave all the territory within the Straits,
is remarkable and suggests a date for the end of Atlantis circa
1220–1186 BC.

Plato's actual words however, are that after the Greeks 'saved
the others from slavery and set them free . . . at a later time there
occurred portentous earthquakes and floods and the island of
Atlantis was swallowed up by the sea and vanished . . . ' and the
date of the war is given, strange as it may seem, as concurrent
with the founding of Athens.

Remember the youths in the labyrinth of Crete sacrificed to the half-bull, half-man, Minotaur. Could it have been these that the Greeks 'saved from slavery and set free'?

Legend says that Theseus led a party from Athens in a raid on Crete in 1400 BC,[39] freeing the Greeks from the oppression of King Minos. Theseus is also credited with the founding of Athens and creation of the first democracy at around this time, 1400 BC.[48]

So here we have the exemplary Athens Plato described 'acting partly as leader of the Greeks, and partly standing alone when deserted by all others'. Should Plato's 9,000 'years' before Solon be in fact lunar months, then this would bring the end of Atlantis down to this period from 1400 BC–1186 BC. A sidereal lunar month of 27.32 days would give a date for the war of 1263 BC – the date of the war against Troy, corresponding as the Egyptian priest said, to 'the noblest of the deeds they (the Greeks) performed'. 8,000 'years' for the Egyptian involvement when similarly converted to sidereal lunar months gives a date of 1188 BC, date of the final defeat of the Sea Peoples and equally the finest of the deeds the Egyptians performed.

This was a period of great upheaval in the eastern Mediterranean and after this time the weakened nations entered into a period of decline marking the end of the Bronze Age. Greece indeed lost the art of writing just as Plato tells us, and this was not regained until the classical era of Plato's own time.

Vase painting from Cyprus showing a Phoenician galley loaded with wine amphorae.

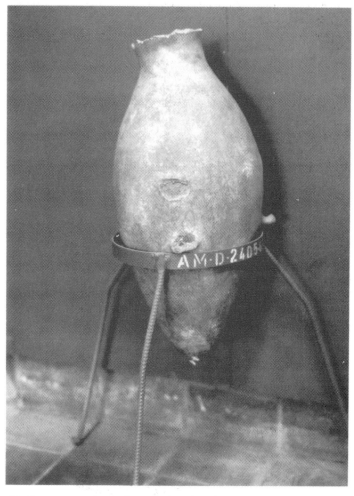

Mediterranean-style amphora said to date from 1200 BC and found in the museum at Oruro, Bolivian Altiplano. Note the similarity to amphorae from Cyprus on opposite page.

The Prince of Knossos, Crete.

Around 1200 BC two of the earliest known civilisations in the Americas began,[10] the Chavin of Peru and the Olmecs of Mexico's Gulf Coast, both of which indulged in the cult of the jaguar.

About this time also, the Valley of Mexico was completely flooded,[9] the water level rose by some 60 ft and may have taken centuries to finally drain away. The archaic civilisation in the area was completely lost and its remains were found in a layer of mud by Zelia Nuttal excavating at Zacatenco in 1900.

Mayan nobleman with plumed headgear.

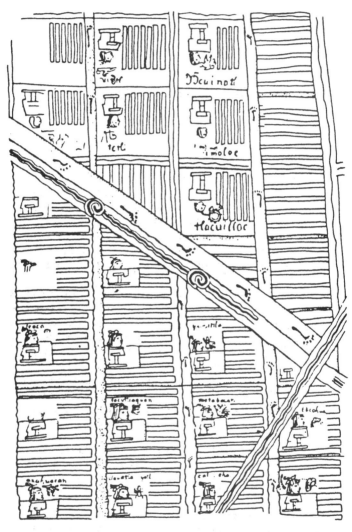

The Aztec system of cultivation illustrated here with its numerous allotments, criss-crossed by canals and transverse canals – a re-creation of the system which originally existed in Atlantis?

CHAPTER 6

Legacy of Aztlan

NO ONE KNOWS for certain where the Aztecs came from. They claimed to come from a place called Aztlan which means the place of whiteness or the place of cranes and is described as an island surrounded by reeds in the middle of a lagoon. From the name Aztlan the name Aztec was taken and in the later migration of these peoples they changed their name to *Mexica*, however scholars of the eighteenth and nineteenth centuries identified them as Aztec by which name they are still known.

In their early travels they settled at Tula, capital of the Toltecs with whom they seem to have had some ancestral connection. One can compare directly one of the colossal statues known as 'Atlantes' found at Tula, Mexico, with similar statues found at Tiahuanaco, Bolivia and the styles are so similar as to suggest a common cultural background.

It is thought that the ancestors of the Central Americans came by sea from the east, but then South America lies to the east of Central America and anyone making a sea passage to Yukatan from South America would arrive by sea *from the east*.

In Yukatan the traditions all point to an Eastern and foreign origin for the race. The early writers report that the natives believed their ancestors to have crossed the sea by a passage which was opened for them. (Landas *Relacion*)

It was also believed that part of the population came into the country from the West, Lizana says that the smaller portion, 'the little descent', came from the East, while the greater portion, 'the great descent', came from the West. Cogullada considers the Eastern colony to have been the larger . . . (*North Amer. of Antiq.*)[16]

'Atlantean' statue from Tula, Mexico. He carries an incense pouch in one hand and an Atlatl (spear thrower) in the other. He wears the traditional feathered head-dress.

Here we have a reference to a colonisation both from the east and the west so it was unlikely to have been an ocean crossing of colonists but rather colonists starting off from the site of their homelands in South America, migrating northwards and travelling by the most practical means arriving by sea.

Statue from Tiahuanaco, Bolivia, in a style similar to those at Tula.

It is said that there were four cities called Tulan, the birthplace of their ancestors being across the sea to the east; when they emigrated to Central America 'they called the stopping place Tulan also; and besides this there were two other Tulans'.

The Aztecs spoke a language called Nahuatl and it was said they had a city of Atlan existing on the Atlantic side of the Isthmus of Panama at the time of the Conquest.

The ancient Mexican legends say that, after the Flood, Coxcox and his wife, after wandering one hundred and four years, landed at *Antlan* and passed thence to Capultepec, and thence to Culhuacan (the crooked mountain associated with Aztlan the island in the lagoon of reeds) and lastly to Mexico.

The Aztecs set out from their home island of Aztlan in a reed-filled lagoon.

When the Aztecs finally arrived in the Valley of Mexico, all the best land was already occupied but they managed to establish themselves on an island in Lake Texcoco which they built up into the island fortress of Tenochitlan, today the site of Mexico City. The city was largely built on reclaimed land, formed by the process of tying bundles of reeds together and covering them with earth to make 'floating islands' called chimpanas which they anchored to the bottom until the roots took hold.

It is thought that perhaps there were two Aztlans.[43]

It must equally be appreciated that Aztlan is as much a concept as a place. The future Tenochitlan was to be in effect another Aztlan, a centre of population by lagoon waters – though it was never to be given that name. The priests gave orders that the nearby river should be dammed; once the dam was made, the waters flowed and spread over all the plain, forming a great lagoon; this they surrounded with willows, poplars and sabines; it became filled with cuperus and reed-mace; it began to be stocked with every kind of fish upon

The city of Tenochitlan at the time of the Conquest. Larger and more
splendid than any in Europe at the time, it contained temples,
pyramids, canals, aqueducts, markets of fresh produce and finely
crafted jewellery etc. Constructed on a carefully chosen site high up
in a mountain valley, was it built in memory of the city of Atlantis –
perhaps the origin of the Aztecs themselves?

earth. Marine birds came, such as ducks, geese, herons, widgeons, with which the whole surface was covered, as well as with many other kinds of fowl, which the lagoon of Mexico today maintains and feeds.

In other words the Mexica (Aztecs) were seeking to reproduce the conditions of their former home, Aztlan as well as those of their future island capital.

The Valley of Mexico itself lies midway between the two seas at an altitude of 7,000 ft. By definition it is not a valley but a basin, since it lacks any natural outlet. It is ringed by a kind of giant horseshoe of mountains on the east, south and west sides. Nowadays the general aspect of the valley is arid and dusty for part of the year owing to the drying up and subsequent drainage of the former great lagoons which covered most of its surface. In their aquatic milieu the Mexica were reverting to the traditional lacustrine pattern of life established in their original home of Aztlan.

After its foundation, Tenochitlan was divided into four districts, a symbolic subdivision respected since ancient times.[43]

The division of the city into four quarters has its parallel of course in the Inca division of their empire into four quarters.

The Aztec environment and choice of site, it would seem, was therefore almost an exact duplication of that which existed on the Altiplano, Bolivia. At one time Lake Uru Uru, just to the north of Lake Poopo, was the home of the ancient tribe of Uru Indians who similarly dwelt amongst reed islands on the lagoon, building reed boats and hunting the wildfowl on the lake.

At the time of the Spanish Conquest under Cortes, Tenochitlan was a thriving city of 300,000 people, criss-crossed with canals and linked to the mainland by three long causeways.

The Conquistadors could not believe their eyes when they first caught sight of the city.

When we saw so many cities and villages built in the water and other great towns on dry land, and that straight and level causeway going towards Mexico, we were amazed and said that it was like the enchanted houses in the legend of Amadis, on account of the great towers and buildings rising from the water, all built of masonry. Some of the soldiers asked whether the things we saw were not a dream? It is not surprising that I describe it here in this way, since there is much to ponder and I do not know how to tell it; for we saw things never before heard of or seen or even dreamed!

The canals were crossed by fortified and removable bridges, which greatly hindered the plundering Spaniards when they attempted to retreat, carrying off the Aztecs' gold and riches, most of which were lost in the lake.

To prevent flooding of the city and avoid pollution of the chimpanas by dissolved salts, a ten mile dyke was built around the perimeter of the city and fresh water from the mountain streams diverted into the area by an aqueduct containing two channels so that one could be cleaned while the other was in use. Surplus water could be let off from this freshwater lake by opening and closing gates in the dyke. Another aqueduct of masonry was built along one of the causeways linking the island to the mainland and the aqueducts crossed the canals by means of what the Spanish called 'hollow bridges'.[9]

Early Spanish map showing the 'Island Continent'.

CHAPTER 7

Land of the Four Quarters

WHEN THE PORTUGUESE first discovered Brazil, they thought they had discovered a vast island which they at first named 'The Island of Santa Cruz',[8] later the 'Land of Santa Cruz'. For some time, ships sailed up and down the Gulf coast, looking for a passage to the west.

Going back in geological time, there was a considerable period when South America actually was an island, after it had split off from Africa and until it had joined up with North America which had split off from Western Europe. In the present day, the Isthmus of Darien with its jungles and swamps hinders communications between the two continents, so any earlier civilisation leaving South America to settle in Mexico may have found it easier to go by sea, which is the traditional route taken by the Olmecs, the first settlers of the Mexican seaboard.

Prior to the ending of the last Ice Age, circa 10,000 BC, the North Pole lay in Hudson's Bay and a vast ice sheet extended as far south as Louisiana.[27]

At the present time the climate of the Altiplano is cold and inhospitable, due to the altitude of the plain which lies 20° south of the Equator. When the Pole lay in Hudson's Bay, the plain lay 10° north of the Equator and at the change of Pole position prior to this (80,000 BC) at 12° south of the Equator. From 135,000 to 80,000 BC when the Pole lay in Yukon,[35] the Altiplano lay directly on the Equator itself and must have possessed a wonderful climate which has gradually deteriorated ever since.

As already noted, from 38,000 to 23,000 BC the southern part of the Altiplano was occupied by a huge inland sea, Lake Minchin, which dried up for a period of 14,000 years until around 9,000 BC when the plain was inundated once more and covered by another

81

huge sea, the renamed Lake Tauca which lasted a further 1,000 years before shrinking into the Lakes Uru Uru and Poopo.[40]

Is it yet another coincidence that the date for the flooding of the Altiplano with the arrival of Lake Tauca matches Plato's date for the end of Atlantis? (due to 'earthquakes and *floods*'). Lake Tauca rose to a height of 12,204 ft, submerging the Altiplano to a depth of over 200 ft. Also at this time, mammoths *were* hunted by natives using obsidian tipped spears, as were horses, of the original, smaller variety and if at that time the Equator were south of the Altiplano this would resolved the mystery of the plain being 'sheltered from the cold north winds', being closer to the ice sheets then covering North America.

From 7,000 BC onwards for a period of six thousand years temperatures were around 2°C higher than at present[42] and if the Altiplano had a more favourable climate in the remote past, it seems unlikely that it would have been left uninhabited by the natives in South America at that time. Indeed, remains of ancient terraces can still be seen in Peru today far above the perpetual snow line so it is evident that the climate must have been considerably better not too long ago.

So either a civilisation existed here which was destroyed by the flooding of 9,000 BC or, could it be that some time after the waters dried up in 8,000 BC, settlements began here which ultimately evolved into a culture which disappeared either at the time of the invasion of Egypt or earlier.

Robert Graves in a footnote to *The Greek Myths* offers the following comment:

> The Egyptian legend of Atlantis – also current in folk-tale along the Atlantic seaboard from Gibraltar to the Hebrides – is not to be dismissed as pure fancy, and seems to date from the third millennium BC. But Plato's version, which he claims that Solon learned from his friends the Libyan priests of Sais in the Delta, has apparently been grafted onto a later tradition; how the Minoan Cretans, who had extended their influence to Egypt and Italy, were defeated by a Hellenic confederacy with Athens at their head.

In another footnote, Robert Graves adds,

> Lake Tritonis, once an enormous *inland sea* that had overwhelmed the lands of the neolithic Atlanteans, has been slowly shrinking ever

since, and though still of respectable size in Classical times – is now reduced to a line of salt marshes.

Again a perfect description of Lake Poopo and its companion Lake Uru Uru.

Jorge E. Hardoy writing in *Pre-Columbian Cities* offers the following comments:

> Lake Titicaca has been drying up for centuries . . . The lake level has dropped 34 metres since the time when the first great South American city was built near its shore. Among the great archaeological sites of America, Tiahuanaco is one of the least known. In the light of present day knowledge, it is difficult to understand why a city would have been situated in such an inhospitable environment. Considering that today the ruins of Tiahuanaco lie 20 kms from the shore . . . Its inhabitants may have come from regions farther south of the lake, as yet little known archaeologically.

It is no surprise that Deanna Swaney[40] tells us:

> The village of Coipasa sits on an island in the middle of the salar (Salar de Coipasa). Just to the north is the amazing village of the Chipaya Indians. This group, which is conjectured to be the remnant of the lost Tiahuanaco civilisation occupies but a single desert village of circular mud huts. The Chipaya language, vastly different from either Quechua or Aymara closely resembles Mayan but some anthropologists note similarities to Arabic and North African tribal languages also.

It has been the practice throughout history to rebuild cities after periodic destruction and it may be that the city of Lake Tritonis was different from the original of Plato. Elsewhere in the Greek Classics we are told that the Atlanteans were at one time defeated by the Amazons who, after obtaining their oaths of allegiance rebuilt their city on a peninsula in a lake.

> It is the country of the Atlanteans mentioned by Diodorus Siculus as a most civilised people living to the west of Lake Tritonis from whom the Amazons seized their city of Cerne . . . Invading the land of the Atlanteans, whose capital is on the Atlantic side of Cerne, Myrine (Queen of the Amazons) defeated them decisively and, crossing over to Cerne, captured the city. She then put every man to the

sword, enslaved the women and children and razed the city walls. When the remaining Atlanteans agreed to surrender, she treated them fairly and in compensation for the loss of Cerne, built the new city of Myrine wherein she settled the captives and all others desirous of living there.

The Amazons incidentally, wore armour made from the tough, scaly skin of 'almost unbelievably large serpents'.

The Amazons, we may recall, were a band of legendary female warriors who made an appearance at the siege of Troy and fought on the side of the Trojans. It was said that they had a breast cut off to facilitate drawing the bow and lived in a society where men were excluded.

Descending the Amazon River, the first Spanish explorers encountered female warriors en route, and thus the river acquired its name. In 1538 Jiménez de Quesada reported:

> When the camp was in the valley of Bogotá, we had news of a tribe of women who lived on their own with no Indian men living amongst them; because of which we called them Amazons. Those who told us about them said that these women became pregnant from certain slaves whom they purchase. If they give birth to a son, they send him to his father; but if it is a daughter they rear her to augment their republic . . . And they were very rich in gold.

One party of Spaniards had had a hard time fighting the Indians.

> We saw ourselves ten or twelve of these women, fighting there in front of all the Indian men as female captains. They killed any who did turn back, with their clubs, right there in front of us, which is why the Indians kept up their defences for so long. These women are very white and tall, with very long braided hair wound about their heads. They are very robust, and go naked with their private parts covered, with bows and arrows in their hands, doing as much fighting as ten Indian men.

The temptation exists, whatever the name of the city on the lake according to the Greek texts, to wonder whether this city with its golden walls, silver, copper and gold pinnacles and temples might not be in fact the same whose name was whispered and revered among the Indians as *El Dorado*. Indeed, a map from the possessions of Sir Walter Raleigh and prepared for him by the Orinoco river Indians shows a large, elongated lake very similar to the Altiplano lake, fed by numerous mountain streams.

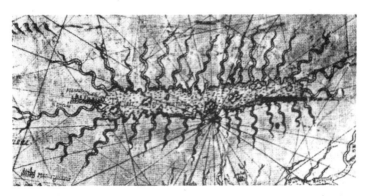

Raleigh's map of Lake Manoa.

Sometimes the story of El Dorado centred around a legendary native chieftain who, after daily anointing his naked body with oil, then had fine gold dust blown onto him so that he became 'the golden man' – *El Dorado* – and would each evening wash the dust off in a mountain lake, thought to be Lake Guatavita, Columbia. At other times it was the land itself which was held to be *El Dorado* and became associated with a large inland salt lake called Manoa. Domingo de Vere claimed to have found it – 'most rich, high, agreeable, with great valleys, with many rich mines of gold and silver and some of iron, and a great saline lake'.

In the north, it was thought El Dorado lay in the south; in the east, it lay to the west and in the south, it lay to the north. Always over the next hill or valley. In Chile, the legend existed of a magical city of gold.

> On the borders of a mountain lake whose whereabouts no one knows, there exists a magic city whose streets and palaces are made of solid gold . . . This golden city will become visible at the end of the world. It is commonly known as the city of Caesars.

The irrigation canals which were a feature of the plain could only function because there was an adequate supply of water in the mountains, and from Lake Titicaca, which previously had a much higher level.

Irrigation canals were also a feature of the Inca landscape. The Inca built up massive irrigated stepped terraces, transporting the earth from other areas to use the most productive type of soil and channelling water across considerable distances. The Inca knew the importance of these water channels and that many of them had been built at a time long before when the country was occupied by a large labour force.

A remarkable book *Letter to a King*,[3] a petition by one of the few remaining Inca noblemen Huaman Poma (1567–1615) to the King of Spain records the details,

> In every village in this country there are watercourses, constructed in ancient times, into which the water is diverted from rivers, lakes or ponds. So much labour was involved that the cost . . . These works date back to the time before the Incas, when there was a large population under a single king. Not only watercourses were constructed but also terraces for the planting of crops on the hillsides. These were built up laboriously by hand, without tools, by Indians who each placed a single stone at a time to make long heaps. The number of workers was so vast that these projects were rapidly completed. Thus the terrain was made to bear cereals to feed the people, even in the sandy coastal plains and the rugged scenery of the Andes. Bridges and aqueducts were built and the marshes drained by order of these early kings.
>
> Then came the Incas, who ordained that existing custom and law should be preserved. There was to be no interference with the irrigation of the orchards and pastures which reached as far as the mountain peaks and gorges. They knew that these works, constructed by so great a labour force, could never in all probability be repeated.

Indeed, when we look around we find other evidence of a vast labour force. Gene Savoy, exploring the Peruvian Andes found the remains of several Great Walls, crossing the coastal deserts in the Andean foothills. The system was served by a road 100 ft wide which led C. N. Griffiths of the *Peruvian Times* to comment, 'If it was designed for armies, they must have been mighty armies.' But then, didn't Plato say the bridges of Atlantis were 100 ft wide!

Remains of irrigation canal in Peru. The size of the canal may be
judged from the scale of the archaeologists in the foreground.

Only one statement from Plato's text could not be readily resolved. That 'this region, all along the island, faced towards the
South' . . . So the generally accepted view is that the plain lay on
the south side of the island.

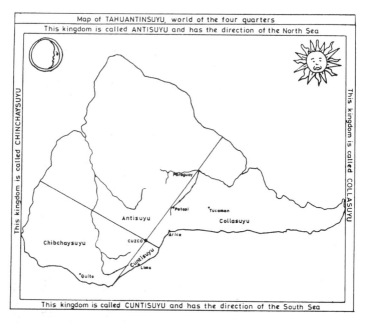

Divisions of the Inca Empire, based on the map by Huaman Poma
(1567–1615). Note that the whole country has been turned on its side
so that, as Plato says, 'this region [the Andes] all along the island,
faced towards the South'; or, as Poma says, 'this kingdom . . . has the
direction of the South Sea'

Huaman Poma has left us a map of the country as the Inca mind
conceived it. In accordance with the ancient practice of drawing
maps so that the direction of the rising sun appears at the top of
the page, the whole continent has been turned on its side, so that
the Andes range appears on what to us seems to be the *south side*,
next to the South Sea while what we would call the eastern side
appears next to the 'Sea of the North'. Adding the word 'sea' after
the direction 'south', would render the passage more comprehen-
sible and read, 'this region, all along the island, faced towards the
South Sea' – which indeed the Andes range does.

The name of the whole country was Tahuantinsuyo, meaning
'the four quarters of the world' and the quarters were named

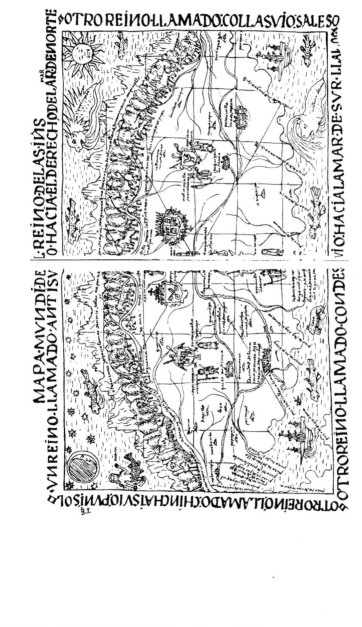

Map of Tahuantinsuyo by Huaman Poma circa 1567–1615.

This kingdom is called CHINCHAYSUYO

This kingdom is called CUNISUYO and has the direction of the South Sea

This kingdom is called ANTISUYO and has the direction of the North Sea

Chibcha
Carib
Arawak
Jivaros
Manao
CHINCHAYSUYO
Chimu
AMAZONAS
Antis
LIMA
Quechua
CUNTISUYO
CUZCO
LA PAZ
ANTISUYO
Tupi
Aymara
COLLASUYO
Pilcomayo
Rio Paraguay
Shavante
RIO DE JANEIRO
Rio Parana
Guarani
SANTIAGO
Puelche
BUENOS AIRES
Tehuelche

The four kingdoms of the Inca Empire
and tribal divisions of South America

This kingdom is called COLLASUYO

Map of TAHUANTINSUYO, Land of the Four Quarters

Map of Antisuyo, part of the Inca kingdoms of Tahuantinsuyo, Land of
the Four Quarters. Note the lands of the Antis, east of Lima.

Megalithic wall at fortress of Sacsayhuaman, near the former Inca
capital of Cuzco, Peru.

respectively Chinchaysuyo in the north, Antisuyo in the east, Collasuyo in the south and Cuntisuyo in the west.

Huaman Poma continues,

> The Indians multiplied like ants or like the sands of the sea until they could no longer find room to live. Then they populated the lower levels of the land, where the climate was temperate and warm. The population was so numerous that it was able to survive a plague which once raged for six months throughout the kingdom. During this period the condors gorged themselves on the human corpses scattered about the fields and villages.

As to the first people to occupy the country, Poma tells us 'the first white people in the world were brought by God to this country. It is said that *they were born in pairs*, male and female, and therefore multiplied rapidly' . . . compare to Plato's statement that Poseidon 'begat five pairs of twin sons and reared them up'.

UNIT OF MEASUREMENT

It remains to be established if a consistent unit of length was used in South America and if so, whether it has any geodetic origins similar to those of other civilisations of the ancient world. Dr Anne Kendall writing in *Everyday Life of the Incas* apparently thinks not since she states 'Inca measurements were surprisingly consistent, based on parts of the human body. In taking measurements they used two sticks as a sliding rule but with an arbitrary unit of measurement.' However, elsewhere in the same book she tells us, 'The coastal road was consistently wide about 5 metres or 16.5 ft in width.'

The standard length of the English surveying pole or rod before metrication was 16.5 ft[31] and this is no mere coincidence since this unit was derived from Sumeria where it comprises 15 Sumerian feet, also found in England and known as 'Saxon feet'. 4 poles made a chain which was divided into 100 links and 40 poles made a furlong of 660 ft. In Sumerian units of course, the furlong was simply 600 Sumerian feet and in this respect is similar to the Greek stadium of 600 Greek feet.

The acre, which comprises 1 furlong × 1 chain and came to be a mysterious 43,560 sq.ft in terms of English feet, was quite simply 36,000 square Sumarian feet.

Gene Savoy gives the standard width of a Chavin column as 500 mm.[14] One wonders whether more accurate measurement might reveal this to be 502.9 mm which would be one Sumerian cubit of 30 shusi. Metric units were known in Ancient Egypt with an Egyptian foot of 300 mm, cubit of 450 mm and royal cubit of 525 mm and other earth commensurate units existed.

Dr Kendall also records a 'fathom' of 65″.

The boundaries of the lands were carefully measured and maintained with markers. A measuring stick based on the 'rikra', a fathom measuring 162 cm or 65 ins was kept for checking land measurements when boundaries were disputed.

This 'rikra' comes close to the fathom of 65.28″ which Prof Alexander Thom discovered as the consistent unit of measurement for the stone circles of the British Isles, comprising two megalithic yards of 32.64″. It also comes close to a unit of 66″ (100 shusi) which would be two Sumerian yards of 33″. This 33″ yard had also been found in parts of Mexico as well as India where it was known as a 'gaz' and contained 25 Indus inches or 50 Sumerian shusi.

In the introduction to *Letter to a King*, Christopher Dilke, author of the English translation, adds the comment, 'It has been my impression that Huaman Poma usually doubled figures relating to time, for whatever cause.'

The cause is probably not that Poma doubled figures but used figures in relation to smaller units. This is consistent with the practice in antiquity of reckoning by units and 'double units', e.g. the smallest unit of Sumerian measurement was the 'barleycorn' of 0.33″ and two barleycorns made the 'shusi' of 0.66″; 100 barleycorns made the yard of 33″ and 100 shusi the double yard of 66″. The Sumerian day consisted of 12 × 'double hours'; the Egyptians counted in tens and their year comprised 36 × 10 days whereas the Maya, who counted in twenties, considered the year as 18 × 20 days.

In order to make the story more agreeable to his readers, Solon attempted to recover the original names before they had been translated into Egyptian and gave what he considered to be the

Greek equivalent. The Greek stadium was derived from the 10th part of a minute of latitude in Greece (although the Greeks of Plato's time were unaware of this[31]) and was divided into 600 Greek feet, equal to 606.8 English feet.

Thus the length and breadth of the plain has been given as 3,000 × 2,000 'stades' but is in fact, as can be measured from the actual size of the plain, 3,000 × 2,000 half-stades of nominally 300 ft, or half-furlongs of 330 ft if we measured to the extreme edges of the plain. An Atlantean 'stade' of 300 ft would be 1/20th of a minute of latitude, also the length, breadth and height of the ziggurat at Babylon and as a pure unit of 300 English feet the distance marched by a soldier in one minute i.e. 60 paces or 120 steps of 30″ – the 30″ step being also the lost 'great cubit' of Ezekiel's temple.

According to *America's Ancient Civilisations* by Hyatt & Ruth Verrill, the smallest Inca unit was a 'yuku' or hand of 5″ with multiples in the 'sikia' of 30″ and 'rikra' of 75″. Should this be so, it has great significance since the hand of 5″ is derived from the decimal division of the Earth's polar diameter i.e. the polar diameter divided by 1,000,000,000 gives a small unit of half an inch of which 10 make the 'hand' of 5″. Five hands make the 'sacred cubit' of 25″, these being the cubits of Ezekiel's temple (Ezekiel 40:5) also that of Revelations 21:16 where 12,000 'furlongs' has been mistranslated instead of 12,000 great cubits (i.e. the perimeter of the city wall in Revelations measured 12,000 great cubits of 30″ which is the same as 14,400 sacred cubits of 25″).

Should evidence of this perfect system of measurement be found here, then perhaps indeed we need look no further for the site of the Garden of Eden.

Certainly the Amazon River is home to the famous Anaconda serpent which can grow to a tremendous length and dislocate its jaw to swallow a large animal.

The natives of the jungle had no need for any form of clothing and instead resorted to daubing colours on their naked bodies as a form of decoration. A form of communal living in large huts containing perhaps eight families was quite normal and as a result of tribal warfare no doubt, there were many more women than men, making this a Paradise for the men who enjoyed the custom of polygamy.

and when he left the woman was free to go with him; if she chose to stay with her husband 'She was not disapproved of, or treated any the worse for this . . . since she had slept with his friend the guest.' Sometimes the women wore a small strip of cloth loosely attached at the waist so that it hung freely, sometimes becoming displaced when they went about their chores or when caught by the wind, but not having eaten of the Tree of Knowledge, to be naked was the natural and preferred state and to be adorned with only an arm or ankle bandage and a few brightly coloured feathers made them in the eyes of some, the ideal of the 'noble savage'.

Coin from Central America.

CHAPTER 8

Nature of Orichalcum

TRANSLATION OF THE word 'orichalcum' seems to have presented some difficulty to both R. G. Bury and Desmond Lee. The word in the original Greek is ὀρείχαλκον, in later Latin it is *aurichalcum* as if 'golden copper'.

In Bury's words,

> Orichalcum was the most precious of the metals then known, except gold . . . They covered with brass, as though with a plaster, all the circumference of the wall which surrounded the outermost circle; and that of the inner one they coated with tin; and that which encompassed the acropolis itself with orichalcum which sparkled like fire.

The footnote is added 'i.e. mountain copper; a 'sparkling' metal hard to identify.'[1]

So we must assume that orichalcum is a natural alloy containing copper. Brass is an alloy of copper and zinc and bronze is an alloy of copper and tin. So by using brass for the outer ring, Bury had left the way open for bronze to be the metal covering the inner ring. But was bronze a 'sparkling' metal?

Pierre Honoré describes the metals of the Andes.[9]

> When the Spaniards invaded the Inca empire . . . they saw objects made of bronze for the first time in America . . . The Inca had learnt how to make bronze alloy from peoples they had conquered, the Aymara and Colla, who had known the technique centuries earlier. They had in turn taken it over from an earlier people, and later created a regular metal industry at Potosi, where their furnaces would glow from the mountains day and night. 'There was such a number of them', the chronicler Coco recorded, 'that the mountains looked as if they were illuminated.'

96

The Inca tribes of Esmeraldes did know alloys, for instance of gold, silver and platinum. Platinum was mined around the Gulf of Guayaquil. The alloy had the 'colour of the silver moon'; it consisted of 70 parts of gold, 18 of silver and 12 of platinum. This alloy is the 'white gold' mentioned on a document on the division of the booty after Cuzco was taken. 'Inca Gold' was an alloy of gold and silver. The alloy which the Spaniards called 'gold of the Andes' was an alloy of copper and gold with a slightly oxidised gleaming surface that can be polished.[9]

Lee considered orichalcum to be 'a completely unknown and imaginary metal'[2] but here we have an alloy, copper and gold, a gleaming metal which sounds very much like orichalcum 'sparkling like fire'.

Orichalcum was 'the most precious of the metals then known, except gold', and yet another wall, a wall of gold surrounded the temple in the centre of the island.

Lee gives the order not as brass, tin and orichalcum, but as *bronze*, tin and orichalcum.[2] We would expect the more common metals to be on the perimeter rings where the circumference was greater and the rarer, more valuable metals to be on the inner rings and on the temple itself. Thus the order becomes copper/tin on the outer ring (copper/zinc according to Bury), tin on the centre ring, copper/gold on the inner ring with a wall of gold surrounding the temple and gold, silver and gold/copper plating the temple walls.

Golden statues were placed inside the temple,

One being that of the God standing on a chariot and driving six winged steeds, his own figure so tall as to touch the ridge of the roof . . . and outside round about the temple, there stood images in gold of all the princes, both themselves and their wives, as many as were descended from the ten kings.

Sheets of gold were also hung on the temple walls by the Inca, who at Cuzco created a garden filled with life-like creatures cast in solid gold and who also maintained golden statues of their ancestors.

At the time of the Spanish Conquest gold was so plentiful in Peru as to be held of little value except as decoration of temples and such, since it was not used as a currency and was held by the

Inca as 'tears of the sun'. The Inca empire was overthrown by Pizarro who landed on the coast of Ecuador in 1531 on a quest for gold, aided by a handful of followers equipped with horses, gunpowder and steel breastplates. Pizarro was able to take advantage of a legend which predicted that one day the bearded gods or Viracochas would return from the sea to reclaim their land, also of the fact that at the time of his arrival a civil war was raging in the country on behalf of two Inca brothers, Atahualpa and Huascar, each contending to be legitimate ruler.

Pizarro met Atahualpa in a walled square in the town of Caja-marca, the Inca having with him no less than 30,000 followers, all unarmed and under strict orders not to attack the Spanish. Pizarro however, had concealed his troops. A Spanish friar presented the Inca with a Bible, which the Inca could not read, neither could he hear, putting it to his ear, any 'words from God' – thus he discarded it, throwing it to the ground, which provided an opportune moment for Pizarro to signal the attack, capturing the Inca and slaughtering his followers.

From captivity, Atahualpa ordered the arrest and murder of his own brother, hoping to consolidate his own position. When Pizarro offered him the opportunity for freedom in exchange for gold, the Inca eagerly agreed to fill a large chamber with gold as high as his arm could reach, tracing a line around the chamber walls.

The word went out to the Empire and the ransom began flowing in, filling the room with gold. The Spanish, on their side, did not keep their part of the bargain and determined to murder the Inca, who was given the choice of being burned to death or garrotted as an alternative if he converted to Christianity.

The Inca opted for conversion and was duly garrotted although at the time a second ransom even larger than the first, was still en route to Pizarro.

Hearing of Atahualpa's execution, his queen ordered the flow of gold to be stopped. Some say it was hastily hidden in the mountains, other reports say it was concealed in a system of tunnels which ran through the Andes, a subterranean road which contained the accumulated riches of the country.

At that time the palaces and temples were customarily hung in gold sheets, the most splendid being the Coricancha in Cuzco where in the west wall the architects had arranged an aperture so that the sun's rays would illuminate the golden wall and the golden sunbeams bounce off certain hieroglyphics and mystic signs at other times invisible.

The signs held the key to the entrance to the tunnel, one entrance being in Cuzco and the tunnel running as far as Lima, then southwards through Bolivia to end in the Atacama Desert in Chile.

Following the death of Atahualpa, the queen gave orders for the tunnel entrance to be sealed with rock and covered over with vegetation. Then she herself committed suicide.

Another entrance was said to exist somewhere on the border between Bolivia and Peru. At a spot on the shore not far from here there was said to be a massive perpendicular stone standing apart from the cliffs of the Andes and known as 'The Tomb of the Inca'. This stone could be seen from seaward and at sunset the rays of the sun lit up certain hieroglyphic characters similar to those in the Coricancha and containing the secret of entry to the tunnels. Near here was a group of three mountains and the entrance to the tunnel lay in one of these mountains on a spur from the main tunnel.[51]

The entire length of the tunnel from Bolivia to Lima and Cuzco was said to contain chambers filled with gold and gem stones but the entrance had been so contrived as to bring an avalanche of boulders upon the unsuspecting trespasser and in any case, was now filled with poisonous gases.

Plato's story is sometimes dismissed as a fable on account of the city walls being plated in exotic metals such as gold and silver, thought to be merely a fanciful embellishment to an already fanciful story. Yet in the Andes we have a later civilisation (the Inca) who continued the practice.

All the metals required to plate the walls and temples of the city of Atlantis are found in the mountains surrounding the plain. Bolivia possesses gold, silver, tin, lead, zinc and copper and sometimes the metals are found occurring together as natural alloys. Potosi with 'glowing furnaces' lies only a hundred miles from the site of the city and Lake Poopo and is famous for its mountain of solid tin, Mount Catavi. Previously it was famous for another mountain, a mountain of silver, most of which was mined for the Spaniards. The first coat of arms, granted to the city by the king of Spain, read 'I am rich Potosi, treasure of the world and the envy

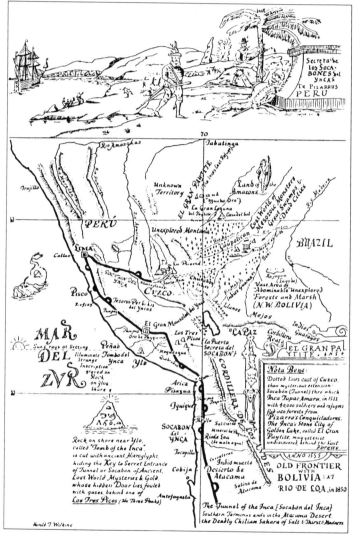

Map of the Andean Tunnel System by Harold T. Wilkins.

The legendary 'Silver Mountain' at Potosi, from a sixteenth-century drawing.

read 'for the powerful Emperor, this lofty mountain of silver could conquer the world'.

From Potosi, the silver was at first transported along the Pilcomyo River which became known as the Rio de la Plata until a Spanish decree ordered the silver to be shipped overland to Lima and thence to Panama in order to develop these two cities. The name Rio de la Plata became preserved in the River Plate, the estuary near Buenos Aires and it is to the Rio de la Plata that one should also look for the legendary city of Tarshish.

After the fall of Atlantis, the metals trade was carried on by the Phoenicians. The Old Testament prophet Ezekiel preaches against the city of Tyre (capital of Phoenicia). He describes their seafaring abilities, calling them merchants for peoples of many isles, and praises their ships built from boards of fir with masts of cedar and sails of fine Egyptian cotton. The ships were caulked by the ancients of Gebel and piloted by the wise men of Tyre, the warships embarking foreign mercenaries. Ezekiel tells Tyre, 'Tarshish was thy merchant by reason of all kinds of riches; with silver, iron, tin and lead they traded in thy fairs.' (Ezekiel 27: 1–12). 'With thy wisdom and with thine understanding thou hast gotten thee riches, and hast gotten gold and silver unto thy treasures.' (Ezekiel 28:4). 'Thou hast been *in Eden* the garden of God; every precious stone was thy covering, diamonds, sapphires, emeralds and gold.' (Ezekiel 28:13).

Of King Solomon we are told (1 Kings 10:22) 'The king had at sea a navy of Thar-shish with the navy of Hiram; once in three years came the navy of Thar-shish, bringing gold and silver, ivory and apes and peacocks.' Had this fleet sailed from a Tharshish near the Guadalquivir River in Spain (near Cadiz) as is presently thought, it would hardly have taken three years and where would they get the peacocks? These magnificent birds originated in India and Ceylon, a long haul from the Mediterranean.

King Solomon built a seaport and a fleet of ships on the shore of the Red Sea manned by the men from Gebel and with the connivance of Hiram of Tyre. I Kings 9: 26–28 has the details . . .

> And King Solomon made a navy of ships in Ezion-geber on the shore of the Red Sea. And Hiram sent in the navy his servants, shipmen that had knowledge of the sea, with the servants of Solomon. And they came to Ophir and fetched from thence gold, four hundred and twenty talents and brought it to King Solomon.

It was Hiram of Tyre who cast all the ornaments for the Temple, the large hemispherical bath with sides five inches thick, supported on twelve brass oxen with bases and wheels etc all in solid brass. It was Hiram who provided all the gold to cover all the walls of the Temple and its oracle and its cherubims etc. It was Hiram who provided Solomon with gold 'according to all his desires'. (I Kings 9:11).

In one year, Solomon made two hundred targets of beaten gold each made of six hundred shekels of gold. Also he made three hundred shields of beaten gold each of three pounds weight of gold. Solomon put them all in the House, together with a throne of ivory overlaid with gold, and the drinking vessels of gold, snuffers, hinges, spoons, bowls, the altar and the table, all of solid gold.

> It was accounted nothing in the days of Solomon. For the king had at sea a navy of Thar-shish with the navy of Hiram; once in three years came the navy of Thar-shish bringing gold and silver, ivory, apes and peacocks.

We must take note that the fabulous source of gold and silver could be reached by Hiram's ships sailing from Tyre on the shores of the eastern Mediterranean and also by fleets sailing from a port on the Red Sea.

Now if a fleet sailed from the shores of the River Plate, it would have followed the trade winds straight across the Atlantic and rounding the Cape of Good Hope carried on and out into the Indian Ocean picking up peacocks in Ceylon and apes and ivories on the coast of India or Africa before entering the Red Sea.

And anyone exporting gold or other metals from the copper and gold mountains of the Andes would need a seaport on the Atlantic seaboard, a site that would be accessible from the ocean and give access to the country's river systems. Thus Tarshish. A sixth century BC description reads . . .

> Tartessus is an illustrious city which takes its name from the river Baetis formerly also called Tartessus. This river has it source in the 'silver mountain' and in its stream it carries, besides silver and tin, a great abundance of gold and bronze. The river Tartessus divides into two arms when it reaches the mouth. Tartessus the city, stands between the arms, as on an island.

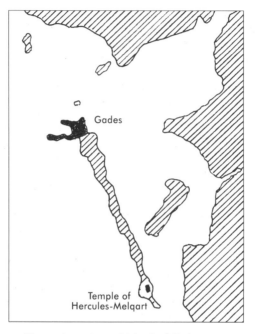

The ancient city and island of Gades, now
modern Cadiz.

Here again we have all the metals of the Andean range and the
'silver mountain' can be none other than Potosi.

Thus Tartessus or Tarshish must have stood at the mouth of the
Rio de la Plata, *the River of Silver* either at its seaward end where
it meets the waters of the Atlantic near Buenos Aires – and it was
rumoured that the Phoenicians possessed a factory town or settlement here – or more probably at the junction of the Pilcomayo
River, as it is now called, with the Paraguay River near Asunción
since this is the farthest point ocean-going vessels could reach
upstream for traffic with the Altiplano.

Indeed at this junction the river does branch into two arms as
per the ancient description and, equally in accordance with the
ancient text, the former River of Silver discharges into a broad
bay – now the Bay of Asunción.

When the Phoenicians visited this hospitable land, it is said they found silver so plentiful that they even cast their ships' anchors in silver in order to carry away as much as they could, and next to the old river of silver we still find marked on a modern map a Rio del Oro – *River of Gold*.

With the collapse of the Atlantis empire, the Phoenicians were able to expand westwards in the Mediterranean, founding a new capital at Carthage around 814 BC. The Phoenicians were also experts in other fields such as canal construction and their expertise was much sought after in the ancient world, being hired by Xerxes to dig a canal through the Isthmus of Acte to ease the passage of his warships for an attack on Greece.

Their own cities they built at specific locations which were easily defensible such as headland promontories or inshore islands providing leeward anchorages a short distance from the mainland such as Gades[56] (a name reminiscent of Gadeira, which Plato said was the name of a kingdom on Atlantis on the part of the continent nearest the Pillars of Hercules). At Gades (pronounced Gad-es) now modern Cadiz (pronounced Ca-dith), they founded the temple to the Phoenician god Melqart, known to the Greeks as Hercules with two columns at the entrance which were sometimes called 'the Pillars of Hercules'.

CHAPTER 9

The Phoenician Navigators

BEFORE THE ADOPTION of Greenwich as the Standard International Prime Meridian, most map makers set the prime or zero meridian somewhere out in the Atlantic Ocean so that it appears to cross the Equator about half-way between the coasts of Africa and Brazil.

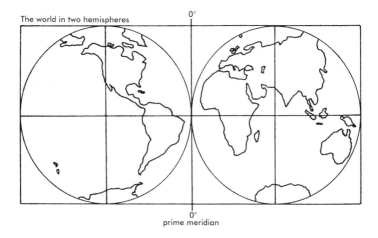

The world in two hemispheres

0°

0°
prime meridian

Now the advantage of having the prime meridian to the west of Africa is that almost all of the 'Old World' can be contained in a hemispherical projection and when the 'New World' was later discovered, geographers found that it too, could be shown in a hemispherical projection, the two being placed side by side.

The configuration of the land masses is such that, leaving aside political boundaries, virtually the same meridians are found convenient for projections today as might have been selected thousands of years ago.

The system of degrees, minutes and seconds was firmly established by the Greek-Egyptian Ptolemy of Alexandria (AD 100–170). Ptolemy as an astronomer and mathematician put forward the 'Ptolemaic or geocentric system' placing the Earth in the centre of the Universe which was to be the accepted model right up to the fifteenth century. His calculation of the size of the world also proved incorrect, making the circumference thirty per cent smaller than a previous calculation which already existed, and it was this smaller circumference which Christopher Columbus used to argue his case for a western sea-route to Asia.

In his work *Guide to Geography* consisting of eight volumes, Ptolemy set out the mathematical principles of cartography referring to places by means of their latitude and longitude and drawing largely on the previous work of the Phoenician geographer, Marinus of Tyre (AD 110).

For his world map, Ptolemy sought to portray the then known habitable lands of the Old World i.e. Europe, Africa and Asia. When questioning travellers and seafarers about the places they had visited, Ptolemy referred them to his prime meridian, that of Alexandria. For his world map however, he set the prime meridian out amongst the Fortunate Isles (now called the Canary Islands and specifically Mt Teide on Tenerife) again following the precedent of Marinus of Tyre.

Any meridian could be chosen as the zero meridian, provided that it is internationally recognised, and each country, be it England, France or Egypt considers that the meridian of its own observatory ought to be the zero meridian.

In England, in the early days of the Ordnance Survey, the zero meridian was established to run through the dome of St Paul's cathedral.

The cathedral of St Pauls was designed and built by the celebrated Sir Christopher Wren on the site of a Saxon church destroyed in the Great Fire of 1666. Not only was Sir Christopher Wren a brilliant architect but he was also one of the foremost astronomers of his day. If ever the reader has the opportunity to visit this famous cathedral, then when he stands under the great dome, instead of gazing upwards, he would do well to look down to the floor. There he will find the largest compass rose in England, set out within a retaining circle bounded by the octagonal symmetry of the massive piers supporting the dome. The circular brass plate in the centre of the floor has a finely engraved north–south line and the peculiar pattern of holes in the plate carries the octagonal motif, although it is difficult to recognise at floor level. Make the 330 ft climb to the platform atop the dome and you will find a small glass observation panel enabling you to look down directly onto the centre of the floor. From here, the 32-point compass design may be seen to better advantage and beneath the brass plate in the centre of the floor lies the crypt with the tomb of Nelson.

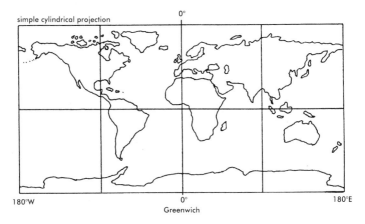

simple cylindrical projection   0°

180°W   0°   180°E
Greenwich

When Greenwich was established as a royal observatory by Charles II, it was geodetically keyed to St Pauls. The cathedral occupies an ancient site on the top of a low hill formerly in the heart of London, and only a short distance opposite near Amen corner is the site of the city gate, the Ludgate, a site now occupied by the church of St Martin within Ludgate. Rebuilt by Wren after the Great Fire and with a spire designed to counterbalance the dome of the nearby cathedral, this now forlorn church is dedicated to a soldier, Martin of Tours, and is none other than the chapel of the Honourable Society of the Knights of the Round Table.

Now the great disadvantage of a prime meridian derived from the arbitrary location of a national capital such as London, is that when we portray the world in a cylindrical projection, the 180° east meridian cuts through the land mass of Eastern Siberia near the Kamchatka Peninsula.

The importance of the 180° east meridian is namely this; it is where *east* meet *west*. Somewhere out here we have to draw a line and ideally we do not want it to be on dry land since some poor soul might find himself on two days of the week at the same time!

Now if we had to start afresh to choose a prime meridian, what unique geographic event would govern our choice?

That unique geographic event, we can see, is the 38-mile wide Bering Strait on the other side of the globe and today the international date line runs through the Strait passing between the islands of Big Diomede and Little Diomede.

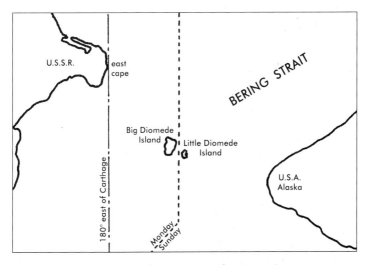

The International Date Line in the Bering Strait.

We choose a line according to the political whims of the day and I would suggest that at one time, a line touching the East Cape, i.e. the easternmost extremity of the land mass of Europe and Asia was chosen. One could thus stand on the shore of the Cape and be in Monday, but set off onto the sea and you find yourself in Sunday!

Bearing in mind that many of the Ancients wrote and read scripts from right to left, the East Cape could then be considered '0' as the first point of the Siberian land masses, working westwards a new 180° or central meridian would be established at a point 10° 20'E of Greenwich and the full 360° circle would meet back at East Cape.

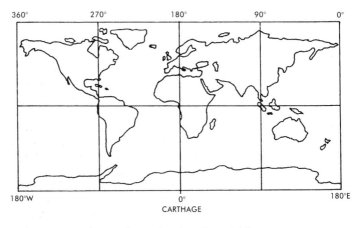

A central meridian based on Carthage.

This new central meridian, which could also be considered a 'zero' meridian, would pass through the island of Elba and touch the North African coast at the site which was to become the capital of the great Phoenician trading empire – Carthage.

The city, whose name actually means 'new capital', was founded by a party of colonists who sailed to the site under the leadership of Princess Dido.

This intrepid lady was at one time, with her brother Pygmalion, joint ruler of Tyre. According to the Greek story, she appropriated the wealth of the city state and consequently her husband was murdered on the orders of Pygmalion. By return, she tricked

Pygmalion into sending her a fleet of ships and then sailed off with the Tyrrian treasure, conveniently calling in at Cyprus to pick up eighty temple virgins before sailing directly to the promontory where Carthage was to be founded.

What greater achievement then, could a maritime nation like the Phoenicians have, than to build their premier city on a unique zero meridian so that it was truly the centre of their maritime empire?

From the origin of the English inch as the 1/500,000th part of the Polar Diameter, and the Egyptian Metric Units, it is evident that someone must have surveyed the Earth to an extreme degree of accuracy in the remote past. But who?

The Great Pyramid of Egypt is considered by some to have been built as a geodetic marker. Its apothem (sloping side) was reputed according to Diodorus Siculus and Strabo to be one stadium long which from ancient writings was considered to be 1/10th of a geographic mile (minute of arc). A 1/6,000th part of a minute of arc gives a geographic foot of 12.15″ and a 1/5,000th part of a minute of arc gives an Egyptian 'remen' of 14.58″ used for land surveying. As the side of a square, the remen gives a diagonal of 20.63″ which is the royal cubit used in the construction of the King's Chamber of the pyramid since its base measures 34.37 ft (20 cubits) by 17.19 ft (10 cubits). The King's chamber also contains the red granite coffer said to have been made in Atlantis.[33]

The Great Pyramid was said to have been built as a repository of ancient wisdom, celestial and terrestrial globes etc and for this reason was broken into in AD 820 by Caliph Al Mamun who reportedly after tunnelling through the softer limestone slabs in order to avoid the granite plugs blocking the entrance passageway, found nothing but the granite coffer already empty and lidless.

In the Egyptian vision of the afterlife there existed the Elysian Fields or 'fields of peace'. Situated on a Paradise Island in the Far West, i.e. over the western sea in the land of the sunset, they were the destination of the souls of the dead and are depicted in the 'Book of the Dead' as a quadrangular plain surrounded by a perimeter canal and intersected by transverse canals like those of the plain of Atlantis. It is sometimes suggested that the Egyptians were formerly a colony of Atlantis. Perhaps the discovery of a hidden chamber in or under the Great Pyramid will ultimately reveal the answer!

A recent Equinox film *The Mystery of the Cocaine Mummies*

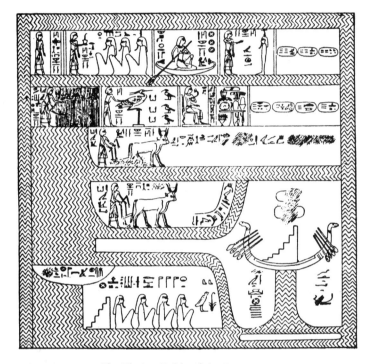

The Elysian Fields of the Egyptians.

presents new forensic evidence that cocaine and tobacco were used in Ancient Egypt as preservative herbs in the mummy of Rameses II who died in 121 BC around the time of the Sea Peoples. Tobacco is a well-known American plant although it is thought that a now lost strain might have existed in Africa. Cocaine, however, only comes from the coca plant found in South America, growing along the slopes of Bolivia, Peru, Ecuador and Columbia.

For the cocaine to arrive in Egypt there must have been a people who cultivated, exported and traded in the plant. These people would have had to cross the Ocean, either the Atlantic to the east, whence they could arrive in Egypt via the Red Sea or through the Strait of Gibraltar, or they would have had to cross the Pacific, a far greater distance, making their first landfall in China where traces of cocaine were found. The coca leaf could then have passed overland via intermediate traders, or ships could simply have sailed via the various islands from South America as far as the Indian Ocean, opening up access to Egypt and Mesopotamia (Plato did in fact say that the travellers of that time crossed from Atlantis to other islands, and from those islands to the great continent beyond.)

It is sometimes said that the Ancients could not cross the oceans since, in their time, the keel had not yet been invented. However, when the Spanish first sailed to Peru they encountered large sea-going rafts sometimes up to 100 ft in length and of 60 to 70 tons displacement. Some of these rafts had bipod masts with large square sails, a hut built on the deck aft, with provision for cooking, water storage etc and could accommodate entire families. Others had two masts with bermudan type sails on curved masts. In both cases the rafts could sail to windward using a type of daggerboard called a *guara* inserted between the balsa logs. The *guara* also served as a rudder and was used in such a way that by simply raising or lowering it the vessel could thus be manoeuvred.

Two Spanish naval officers of 1736 give the details . . .

> The greatest singularity of this floating vehicle is that it sails, tacks, and works as well in contrary wind as ships with a keel, and makes very little leeway. This advantage it derives from another method of steering than by a rudder; namely by some boards, three or four yards in length, and half a yard in breadth, called *guaras* which are placed vertically, both at the head and at the stern between the main beams, and by thrusting some of them deep in the water, and raising others, they bear off, luff up, tack, lay to, and perform all the other motions of a regular ship. An invention hitherto unknown to the most intelligent nations of Europe . . .

Having crossed the great oceans they would naturally wish to return and for this they would require a knowledge of navigation and would presumably embark on a process of making maps and charts for the seas. Pacific voyagers however were known to cover vast inter-island distances, using only oral tradition and navigating by the headings of particular stars.[47]

The Egyptians waited for the rising of particular stars to mark the passage of time. They used 36 of these special stars known as

Decans to subdivide their calendar into 10 day periods. At night the appearance of individual Decan stars over the horizon was used to calculate the 'hours'.

When we see the moon in the sky, we think of the full moon changing to a crescent shape then back to a full moon. We normally think of a month as the interval between full moon and full moon, i.e. between phases of the moon, and this is the normal lunar month which is called a synodic month and consists of 29.53 days. Its apparent motion in the sky is caused by the Earth's rotation and since the moon itself travels on its orbit in an easterly direction it gradually gets left behind since it takes 25 hours to orbit the Earth completely. The time taken for the moon to return to the same position relative to the stars is called a *sidereal* lunar month.

Empires of Time[46] explains the sidereal lunar month. 'A sidereal month (27.32 days) is the time it takes the moon to move from a given constellation all the way around the zodiac back to that same background pattern of stars.'

If this is the unit of Plato's 'years', then it may also be the key to the ancient system of navigation.

A sidereal month cannot be detected by marking out successive moons. Because of the 1/3rd day leftover interval after the 27 day count, the moon's reappearance in the same constellation of the zodiac happens about eight hours (1/3rd day) later. Suppose I begin my first sidereal month by witnessing the moon in a constellation of the zodiac at midnight. The next time around this same event will occur is at eight o'clock in the morning – that is, during daylight, when the stars are not even visible. But if I were to reckon sidereal intervals in groups of three, then I could see a visible moon against the same star pattern at the same time of night, because the third multiple of the sidereal month is a whole number: that is 3×27.32 = 82.

The Inca, it would appear, counted time in *sidereal months*,[46] not only that but they counted in blocks of three months as described above so that each year consisted of 328 days and each quarter comprised 82 days or a double unit of 41 *ceques*. The imperial city of Cuzco was set out on a system of 41 invisible lines radiating from the Coricancha or Temple of the Sun, said to have been sheathed in over 700 sheets of gold and the geodetic heart of Tahuantinsuyo, Land of the Four Quarters.

The Inca and the early inhabitants of South America were in an ideal location for lunar and stellar observations[47] since the continent runs north-south over an extensive range of latitude. Mesoamerican mathematics were based on multiples of the number 20 and it can be no coincidence that the Saros cycle of lunar eclipses repeats itself every 20 'Inca' years.

All over Western Europe are megalithic circles which were used to study the motions of the moon.[52] It can be no coincidence that the Phoenicians chose the site of Carthage and built it on a unique meridian which was the ideal central meridian for a world map. It suggests or even proves, that they could calculate longitude at a remote time long before the problem of longitude became prominent in the western world.

When Columbus opened up the route to 'America' the favoured method of sailing was to sail to a line of latitude (lines of latitude are parallel to the Equator) and follow that line of latitude by dead reckoning (measuring or guessing) the distance travelled until one came to one's destination.

When ships returned to England from the West Indies they found themselves in great peril on approaching the shore. In the year 1707 a fleet of ships returned to England from Gibraltar and three of them ran aground on the rocks of the Scilly Isles with the loss of all hands except one. In total, four ships of the fleet were lost as a further ship managed to refloat but the total loss of life was nearly 2,000 men. The public was shocked, and longitude became the topic of debate until in 1714 it was raised in the Commons, Sir Isaac Newton proposing that the principal methods of determining longitude would depend upon (a) use of an accurate chronometer to keep time (time changes 1 hour for every 15° of longitude, therefore if an observation of a star takes place at Greenwich at 1200 hours and a man on board ship observes the same event at 1 p.m. the seaman must be 15° west of Greenwich).

Method (b) proposed by Sir Isaac Newton was by observation of eclipses of the satellites of Jupiter but due to lack of appropriate telescopes considered not practical, and method (c) was by the place of the moon, but in his day the exact theory was lacking.[54]

The House accepted the report and a bill was passed offering a reward of £20,000 for anyone who could come up with an accurate method to determine longitude at sea. After many trials, the chronometer invented by John Harrison proved successful although he had to wait until personal intervention by King George III secured him his final rewards – he was then 80 and died three years later.[54]

The chronometer of course became the standard method of calculation (combined with observation) and the lunar method completely forgotten. Yet in 1514 John Werner of Nurnberg had proposed a lunar-distance method 'using the Moon as a giant celestial clock, with the Moon as the hand and the stars in the Zodiac as the figures on the dial.'[54]

Little could he have imagined that it had all been done before.

Perhaps the early Atlantean voyagers used a similar system of stellar observation to calculate their position relative to the stars known to reoccur at fixed lunar intervals over their own meridian of origin.

It has been suggested that the famous Piri Reis map which shows part of the American coastline as well as Antarctica is derived from an ancient conical projection centred on Egypt. The Egyptians themselves possessed a system of large global units of 15,000 royal cubits called 'atur', but they had no particular reputation as travellers or seafarers.

The Atlanteans however, had. After the fall of their empire or shall we say, the defeat of the Sea Peoples in 1200 BC, a new power arose in the Eastern Mediterranean, the Phoenicians. They lived in the coastal strip now known as Lebanon and their first city was Byblos where the 'phonetic' alphabet was invented, but are said to have originated from the south of Arabia, or Mesopotamia.

The first civilisation of Mesopotamia was the Sumerian. They created writing in wedge shaped characters called cuneiform, were skilled workers in gold, silver and bronze, invented the wheel, were masters of canal construction and built the first known cities including Ur on the banks of the Euphrates, itself called by the first settlers 'Urutu', meaning Copper River. At Ur, copper daggers, helmets, spears, a double axe of electrum and an exquisite dagger of gold with a lapis lazuli handle have been found dating to 3,000 BC. In the beginning the early settlers lived amongst the marshes and used reed boats not unlike those of Lake Titicaca and formerly Lake Uru Uru. Their traditions included the story of the flood, written by Gilgamesh, ancient king of Uruk and the origin of the flood story of Genesis.

Thor Heyerdahl proved that a reed boat built on the shores of

Africa (to a traditional design by boatbuilders from Lake Titicaca) could cross the Atlantic from east to west. But did anyone ever consider that the first reed boats may have crossed from *west* to *east* perhaps following the route from the River Plate eastwards across the Atlantic, past the Cape of Good Hope and via the Indian Ocean to enter the Persian Gulf and Red Sea to found the early civilisations of Mesopotamia and Egypt?

A boat-shaped formation found near Mt Ararat[52] in Turkey suggests that it could be the fossilised remains of an ancient reed vessel. The outline in plan form is similar to the lines of a giant reed ship and its length corresponds approximately to that of the Ark as described in the Bible.

David Fasold, who measured the site, quotes a previously measured length of 492 ft but he himself considered it to be around 538 ft overall and 515 ft internally, trying to justify the length in Egyptian cubits of 20.62″ in order to make it correspond to the Bible length of 300 cubits.

Thor Heyerdahl, writing in *The Tigris Expedition* states that ancient Sumerian reed ships could carry cargoes of up to 18.5 metric tonnes of copper and that Ur fulfilled a role as port of entry for copper into Mesopotamia. The reed ships could also carry huge quantities of cattle and goods and the ship of Utu-Nipishtim (the equivalent of Noah) had nine inner compartments and six superimposed decks.

These Sumerian ships were known as Ma-gur and Heyerdahl quotes the length as typically 120 *gur* or 300 *gur*. Now if the *gur* was the Sumerian cubit of 19.8″ then the ship would measure some 495 ft, the same more or less as the fossilised remains found near Mt Ararat.

David Fasold had difficulty with the beam, since the Bible quotes a height for the Ark of thirty cubits and a breadth of fifty cubits. Fifty Sumerian cubits of 19.8″ would give a beam of 81.25 ft whereas Fasold measured a beam of 138 ft.

Thor Heyerdahl's reed boat *Tigris* consisted of two large reed cylinders lashed solidly together. But David Fasold found that the 'Ark' vessel contained a 'hull pool' or gap in the centre measuring 200 × 26 ft wide. This suggests the vessel could have been made up of two reed cylinders woven together at the stem and stern but with a gap separating the reed hulls in the centre and this gap could have accommodated a timber structure which in turn would allow for the nine inner compartments or decks of Utu-Nipishtim and additionally allow heavier cargoes to be placed lower down. To build such a vessel, the breadth of fifty cubits is the distance from centre to centre of each of the reed hulls and correspondingly the breadth of the deck they support, which does not project out over the curving sides.

The height of thirty cubits is also the proportionate height of the reed cylinders in a vessel of this type and again, the height of the deck they support.

The Sumerians were said to have arrived by sea, bringing with them a ready made civilisation and some sources suggest they came via the Indus Valley, which itself may have been a staging post for their travels. The island of Dilmun, thought to be modern Bahrain, was the centre for importation of metals, timbers and other goods and Heyerdahl found remains of stone walls whose lower levels comprised interlocking stones similar to those of Andean construction.

The Sumerians were thought to have first settled in Dilmun after the flood,[53] but we must note that another Dilmun exists near the site of the 'Ark' close by Mt Ararat and an Assyrian text says the flood survivors were told to 'Go and dwell in the distance, at the mouth of the rivers', meaning the mouth of the rivers Euphrates and Tigris. The region between these rivers was called Mesopotamia meaning just that, 'the land between the rivers' and great civilisations arose here. Yet it is a curiosity that the latitude of this Mesopotamia, 33° North has its counterpart near the River Plate in South America – latitude 33° South and also known as *Entre Rios*, Mesopotamia or the land between the rivers!

Evidence of a flood was found in Mesopotamia in 1929 by Sir Leonard Woolley digging beneath the deepest levels of civilisation. He found a layer of mud between ten and thirteen feet thick and beneath that remains of earlier cities. But was this a Universal Flood and did the displaced peoples truly know where they originated from?

The Phoenicians were of a red colour and famous for the weaving of a fine cloth which they dyed using a purple dye extracted from the murex shell. They were given the name Phoenicians by the Greeks, meaning dark red or purple. They were Semites and akin to the Hebrews, who called their country Canaan. Both the Canaanites and the Israelites, according to the Bible, were descended from

Lake Uru Uru near Oruro.

The Chipaya village, near Salar de Coipasa,
Oruro province.

Lake Poopo – now receding due to lack of water.

View across canal section with water still in base despite the dry season. The width is almost 600 ft from the far ridge to the point from where the photograph was taken.

The author standing in the base of the canal.

The level plain enclosed by mountains.

A photo-montage giving a view across the plain from the nearby volcano. The canal can be seen continuing across the view from left to right.

Noah, the Hebrews later migrating from Ur to the land of Canaan where they occupied the Plain of Jordan whilst the Philistines occupied the coastal strip south of Phoenicia bordering on Egypt.

It seems probable that the Phoenicians absorbed some of the remnant of the Sea Peoples, thus gaining the necessary navigational skills which enabled them to expand westwards founding Gades and Carthage with its circular dock which could accommodate 220 warships in covered sheds – reminiscent of Atlantis perhaps – and establishing colonies in all the territories described by Plato as being those of Atlantis i.e. North Africa, Spain, Sicily, Ibiza, Minorca etc.

They also acquired the sea routes which enabled Hiram of Tyre in 955 BC to furnish Solomon with the desired metals to plate the walls of the Temple, walls overlaid with the gold of Atlantis.

Like the later American Aztecs, they practised human sacrifice, killing 3,000 prisoners at Himera (Sicily) in 490 BC and infant sacrifices were also numerous – at Carthage infants were committed to the arms of a bronze statue so that at the appropriate moment they might fall into the flames.

In the end it was Carthage itself which succumbed to the flames. After the famous campaign by Hannibal who led a Carthaginian army through Spain to defeat the Roman armies in Italy, the Romans ultimately crossed over to North Africa where they conquered Carthage, razing the city to the ground in 146 BC and assimilating its territories into the Roman Empire.

One explorer who was convinced that South America had an early civilisation unknown to history, was Colonel P. H. Fawcett. Colonel Fawcett was originally seconded from the British army to survey and determine border frontiers in an area adjoining Peru, Bolivia and Brazil. He travelled extensively through unknown territories, listening to the tales of the Indians and reports of fabulous cities hidden in the interior. In Fawcett's words,

> The existence of the old cities I do not for a moment doubt. How could I? I myself have seen a portion of one of them – and that is why I observed it imperative for me to go again. The remains seemed to be the outpost of one of the bigger cities, which I am convinced is to be found, together with others, if a properly organ-

ised search is carried out. Unfortunately, I cannot induce scientific men to accept even the supposition that there are traces of an old civilisation in Brasil. I have travelled much in places not familiar to other explorers, and the wild Indians have again and again told me of the buildings, the character of the people, and the strange things beyond.

One thing is certain. Between the outer world and the secrets of ancient South America a veil has descended.

In 1925 Colonel Fawcett set out on what was to be his last expedition, a trek across central Brazil in search of a city reportedly found by a gang of bandeira as early as 1753. From this trip Colonel Fawcett was never to return and his prophetic words are taken from his diary . . .

Whether we get through, and emerge again, or leave our bones to rot there, one thing's certain. The answer to the enigma of ancient South America – and perhaps of the prehistoric world – may be found when those old cities are located and opened up to scientific research.

That the cities exist I know . . .

CHAPTER 10

Expedition Atlantis

THE PLANE FROM Miami touched down at El Alto airport, La Paz, Bolivia. Altitude 12,990 ft above sea level. It was 5 a.m. and cold. I had had the rabies shots in case I got bitten by a mad dog. The hepatitis 'A' to ward off unsafe food microbes. The cholera jab which I was told was just a formality in case the officials would not let me in without the certificate. I was assured by the medics the inoculation was of little practical effect anyway.

The ticket, a one-way from London Heathrow via Miami. The intention, after Bolivia to continue out through Chile and return via Argentina. Would the officials let me in without a return ticket I wondered, waiting my place in the queue. With no formalities and hardly a glance the officer stamped my passport with a one month visitor's visa, 'Welcome to Bolivia' he said.

I stepped out of the airport, bags in hand into the crisp Altiplano air. Was it really true, after fifteen years dreaming about this trip here I was at last. On the threshold of an adventure to look for evidence in support of my theory that the fabled lost city of Atlantis lay beneath the waters of the salty Lake Poopo a hundred and fifty miles due south on the Bolivian Altiplano.

'Taxi, Señor?' The *taxista* took hold of my cases and threw them into the back of his cab and we were off. The air didn't seem thin at all. What did they mean about altitude sickness? It just seemed like any other place but somehow exhilarating as we entered La Paz and I saw for the first time the host of little houses clinging to the valley sides and the spires of two medieval churches in stark contrast to the towers of the modern skyscrapers.

Would we find an hotel open at this time of day? The *taxista* knew of one near the bus station. That seemed a good idea – I was later to realise what the guide book meant by 'a hefty huff and a puff uphill from the town centre'.

Atlantis – the city beneath the sea. Plato's exact words were 'The island was swallowed up by the sea and vanished'. Taking his word for it that the city had *vanished*, there seemed little point in looking for evidence of the city itself in Lake Poopo but a large part of Plato's description was about the level plain and the huge irrigation canal one stade (600 ft) wide which he said ran right round the plain and back to the sea.

Now if a section of canal could be found remaining to this day in what is now a desert and which happened to be 600 ft wide as per Plato's description, surely this must be the ultimate proof, short of locating the city itself, of the truth of Plato's story.

I already had satellite photos which showed such a section of canal to the north-west of Lake Poopo and just before leaving London had obtained a new edition of a 500,000 scale map which showed a portion of the canal as a *laguna* (lake) in the desert. My first plan was to visit the Instituto Geographico Militario in La Paz to see if I could obtain better quality aerial photos of this canal section before heading off towards Oruro and the edge of the desert.

So day one I started off down the hill past the bus station with its ticket touts and interminable cries of 'O-ru-ro' and 'Co-cha-bam-ba' and down to the city where the maze of streets appeared to have absolutely nothing in common with the page of map I had torn from the guide book.

I saw for the first time the bowler hatted native women squatting in the street selling anything from bubble gum to hot meals for one *Boliviano* (about 15 pence English money). The bowler hats, incidentally, were introduced by one of the Spanish kings as a means of identifying the individual native tribes as a precaution against a possible rebellion. The tradition remains to this day amongst these Andean women otherwise swathed in reams of cloth and with infant babies strapped to their bodies and faces bronzed from the Altiplano sun.

By curious good fortune right in the centre of town, I found a little shop which was the agency for the Instituto Geographico Militario, but it turned out the aerial photos were not kept here but in a building on the other side of town. The lady running the shop gave me a card with the name and address of the Instituto printed on it.

Everything seemed to be going downhill. In the town that was. It was a bright sunny day and everything seemed wonderful and unbelievable. I ended up on the side of a vast gorge spanned by a suspension bridge, the approach guarded by local police in army style uniforms. The immense chasm below was totally breathtaking and perched on a little plateau on one of the cliff sides was a rustic cabin of the sort I had always romantically dreamed of living in! In the exactly opposite direction and way in the distance was the snow capped peak of Illimani. Spectacular is an understatement.

I eventually located the site of the Instituto but it turned out to be *inside* an army barracks. A small side door in the high wall appeared to be the entry and the armed soldiers were checking passes. When my turn came I asked in Spanish if I could visit the Instituto Geographico Militario, holding up the card and pointing to the name and address of the Instituto printed on the card. The young soldier looked at me and the card; looked at the other sentry smiling as if they had some private joke, then shrugged as if he had never heard of the place. After a while he said 'Wait here a moment.' Some scruffy German backpackers got the same treatment. Just when our patience was about to run out, we were told by the guards, 'The sergeant says come back in two hours.'

That was that. Nothing more could be done for the moment except to walk about and fill in the time. At the end of the same street was a huge traffic roundabout and in its centre, a reconstruction of the semi-submerged temple at Tiahuanaco. Worth a visit. In the centre of the walled courtyard stood a giant statue brought from Tiahuanaco. This was what I wanted to see as it was similar in style to the statues known as 'Atlantes' found at Tula in Mexico and the Aztecs came via Tula before founding their capital Tenochitlan (now Mexico City) on an island in Lake Texcoco. The Aztecs claimed to have come from an island called *Atzlan* and if they had statues similar to those at Tiahuanaco . . . the connection seemed obvious.

Set into the walls of the temple courtyard were copies of stone heads which later I found out were meant to represent the chieftains of all the different nationalities who came to visit Tianuanaco. The reconstructed temple now formed a charming 'garden' filled with all kinds of stone relics although entry was barred by a metal gate.

Back to the barracks and this time no sign of the Germans. 'Come back tomorrow at 09.30' the sentry said. Another disappointment. Friday, next day, 09.30 *en punto* I presented myself again at the barracks. Same routine. I could see an immaculately dressed officer in a greatcoat pacing up and down inside the entrance looking over the people waiting to get in. Lots of high ranking officers were coming and going all in equally immaculate uniforms. It reminded me of the smartness and correctness of military behaviour.

'Come back Monday morning,' said the soldier on duty with a broad smile. It must have seemed like a huge joke for them.

The sights and sound of La Paz were something not to be missed. So many little side streets, everywhere photocopy shops – it seemed like some kind of craze and the copies were ultra cheap. Bazaars full of alpaca garments, leather bags and all the usual tourist stuff. The street vendors with their bowls of soup, flaming kebabs and best of all, the glasses of freshly squeezed orange juice again one Boliviano. In Spain, everything from bus fares to coffee had been a uniform 125 pesetas, but here it was one Boliviano. It reminded me of a scene from an old-time western where everything cost one dollar making a 'one dollar' town. This was a 'one Boliviano' town.

The nights were cold but then I was on the cold side of the hotel, i.e. in the shadow and overlooking the bus station and awakened each morning with the sharp cries of 'O-ru-ro'.

Monday. It dawned on me to dress a bit better. No more the torn and worn jacket bought thirteen years earlier in Mallorca which I usually wore trying to look inconspicuous in the crowd (impossible anyway as a 6′ 3″ *gringo* in a land of short native Indians!) Instead my best brown leather jacket, Farah trousers, brown leather shoes highly polished that morning by a shoe shine boy for one Boliviano and of course a shirt *with a tie*.

09.30 again at the side door of the barracks. I asked for the Instituto. If this didn't work I intended to phone them and make an appointment. I could see the officer nodding then he disappeared. '*Si Señor*' was the reply. 'Come this way.' I stepped into and through the guardroom. 'Leave your passport at the control.' With great reservations I handed my passport to the sentry at the

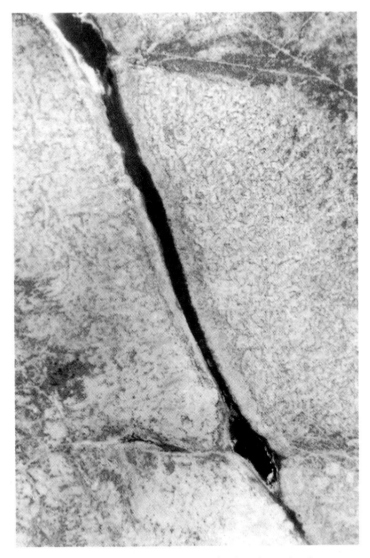

Aerial photograph of canal section, 600 ft wide, in the desert
north-west of Lake Poopo.

window. Would I see it again I wondered? Well with all those machine guns they could have taken it anyway. I was given an ID tag and told the Instituto was across the square. Progress!

I found the Instituto with a huge model theodolite on the roof. Another checkpoint. More armed sentries. Again I asked to visit the Instituto holding up the card with the name printed on it and again the same blank look from the sentry as if it never existed while the Instituto's name was written in large letters just above his head on the side of the building.

Just then the officer stepped forward. The soldiers shrank away like rats before a flame and the officer waved me through and took me inside to the archive room where I was assigned an assistant to search the air photo files.

The site in the desert was not easy to identify at first since the air photos were not plotted onto maps but recorded as flight numbers and aircraft tracks with random place names quite different from those on the modern map. Shuffling through piles of photos, one of them stood out immediately with a huge 'scar' running north to south – this was the section of canal I was looking for.

The prints were ordered and obtained the following day but the combination of food poisoning and altitude sickness finally laid me low and I spent a further day in the hotel before setting off for Oruro.

Located a hundred and fifty miles or three hours by bus south of La Paz, Oruro is a large mining town and community on the edge of the desert and the closest town to the site of the canal feature and the site of the city which presumably lies beneath Lake Poopo. Frequent buses leave La Paz and the route in general is quite a pleasant one down the broad valley which opens out at Oruro onto an extremely flat plain steeped in rich colours with numerous volcanic peaks in the far distance. At first sight Oruro appears like a shanty town – the guide book says 'You will either love it or hate it' but, in fact, it is quite a pleasant and large city with an impressive and charming main square in-cluding a 'gold' statue in honour of the man who brought the railway.

At Oruro I hired a taxi for a drive to the outskirts of the town to see Lake Uru Uru which was indeed a beautiful sight with its pink flamingoes and my first true glimpse of 'the level plain en-closed by mountains' as Plato described it. We went as far as the guard post on the outskirts of Oruro which was as far as the taxi could go, then returned to Oruro.

In Oruro I walked past the market, explored the bus terminal and rail station which again was like something out of a wild west movie, expecting at any moment some old steam train to come clanking in and Butch Cassidy himself to step out amongst clouds of steam from the rear of the train, but nothing moved at Oruro and it seemed not so much at which *hour* a train might arrive but on what *day* a train might arrive.

I also found that due to the altitude I could hardly walk more than a few yards without being out of breath and having to stop for a rest. Someone suggested some 'altitude pills' from the chemist, which was in any case closed, but one of the locals merely laughed and said it would wear off after a few days, 'Try some coca tea', he said.

Back in La Paz I changed rooms to the sunnier side of the hotel and things seemed much better. I had a contact phone number for one of the leading archaeologists in the area so gave him a call and was invited to meet him at his house.

He was a most charming gentleman and listened patiently to my explanation of the canals etc and it was his final conclusion that tipped me in favour of a return to Oruro – 'But you've got to see it for yourself' he said and so it was. A week later I was back in Oruro.

I checked in at the Hotel Terminal and asked the porter about vehicle hire, 4WD that is. '*No problema Señor*' and he gave me the number of Rent-a-Car.

One phone call and one hour later I was in the office of Rent-a-Car and at first it seemed that all the vehicles were booked up for the coming fiesta that weekend. I would have to wait till Tuesday. But maybe if I called back in two hours it might be possible. . . And possible it was, thanks to the good efforts of the proprietor. Next morning I was at the office at 08.15 and there was the jeep with driver.

We bought some spare gasoline, sandwiches and a giant bottle of orange drink on the way out of town and after paying a small fee at a frontier checkpoint we were speeding down the road to the desert village of Toledo.

Before leaving Oruro I had made a note of the vehicle's mileage since the plan was to navigate using the mileometer. After a few miles the driver drew my attention to the speedometer. I looked. What was I supposed to see? *'No funciona'* he said – 'It's not working.'

That seemed like the end of it before we had even started. How would we know where to turn off the main road to find this canal in the remote desert?

We sped on through Toledo. In this tiny obscure village, concrete had yet to be invented and the main square was just a red dirt plaza and the road itself a dusty red track. Finally we came to the junction where the map showed a road branching off to the left.

The driver stopped the vehicle. At a collection of little huts he asked 'Is this the road to Andamarca?' Grins and nods and a few waved hands confirmed that it was so we followed the track off to the left and descended onto the level Altiplano. Suddenly there was no more track and just desert. It reminded me of the title of a book by Col. John Blashford-Snell, *Where the Trails Run Out*. Now I knew what he meant.

With no navigational equipment and only a 1/500,000 scale air navigation chart we headed off in the direction of Andamarca. The driver seemed to know the way and that's where he thought we were going.

After a spell I asked him how many kilometres he thought we had travelled. 'About 20 kms' he replied. I didn't really believe him. That would have meant we were way past the canal site. Just then we forded a broad stream and fortunately it was shown on the map – I knew where we were. We had actually gone only about 6 kms!

Shortly afterwards we crossed a *salitre* – a branch of the salt desert – then soon afterwards another *salitre*, both shown on the map. Back on the main trail again I felt it was time to head off eastwards and turned left into the bush. We found a track leading to a supposed quarry and followed this as far as we could go. Then indeed the trail ran out. We left the vehicle and saw some farmers herding llamas.

'Any signs of a *laguna* near here?' we asked. *'No Señor, no hay lagunas aqui'* (no lakes or lagunas here) was the reply but I knew we had to be in the right area.

We walked eastwards over the sand dunes and up a gently inclined and graded slope and suddenly found ourselves on the ridge of an embankment.

There it was. The *laguna* as shown on the map, a narrow ribbon of water remaining in the base of the channel (it was the dry season) and the channel itself had a flat base with gently sloping sides.

I congratulated the driver on our extremely good fortune in finding the site, took a few photos north and south and set out to climb the opposing ridge, pacing out the distance on the way up. I made it about 230 ft which together with a base of around 120 ft made the overall width just under 600 ft or one stadium from crest to crest – as Plato said, 'It seems incredible that it should be so large as the account states, but we must report what we heard . . . the breadth was one stade.'

Back in the centre of the channel a wild dog appeared from nowhere and began snapping at my heels – the nightmare scenario of being bitten by a dog in the middle of the desert distracted me from my thoughts of making any more measurements and, although I had already had the rabies shots, had no wish to try out their effectiveness!

So we headed back to the jeep and returned to the main route with the intention of finding another section of canal further south to see if its construction was consistent with the section we had just visited.

About three miles further south we again turned left and headed off into the bush, again using the vehicle as far as it would take us. This time after leaving the jeep we walked quite a way eastwards until we came to a sort of valley or irregular depression but not anything like the feature we had seen to the north. It seemed disappointing and I did not wish to drag the driver any further off into the bush. 'Wait here, I'm just going a little further. Be back in five minutes' I said.

Thirty minutes later I came across the canal feature proper and was able to pace out the base of about 120 ft without being molested.

I returned to find the driver patiently sitting on a sand dune and we only had one more task I could think of – to climb the nearby volcano for a better view!

A few more miles to the south and we were abreast of the volcano. After a false start jolting over some horrendous rough ground full of pot-holes and gulleys, we found a trail which appeared to lead to the top and continued enthusiastically in the vehicle. The trail turned to rocks and the rocks turned to boulders until there was a final metallic 'clunk' and that was it. We had stopped.

We both got out and I set off on foot to climb to the top leaving the driver to sort out the damage. From the top one could see the level Altiplano extending in all directions both west and eastwards. To the east the canal had left a salt trail running right across the desert and in the distance the dried up Lake Poopo glared white from its salt deposits. I took a horizon to horizon panoramic series of overlapping photos. On my return I found the driver had backed the vehicle down to a level turning point. With the aid of a giant hammer and a 5 ft crowbar loaned from a local villager he had restored the jeep to its former state of readiness and soon we were back on the main road heading once more towards Oruro.

CHAPTER 11

Conclusion

IT WAS NOW 1995 and fifteen years since I had completed the typescript of my book on ancient measurements which I deposited at Stationers' Hall copyright registry on 4 July 1980. Two of those chapters had proposed that the Altiplano was the site of Atlantis and I had imagined that all the world would be clamouring to learn of the site of the lost city. Instead passed many years of frustration of literally not being able to give the idea away. One supporter in the early days had been Colonel John Blashford-Snell who had shown an interest in the project and intended to take his Young Venturers there but, because of political difficulties, had called the venture off.

I had met him through an introduction from Egerton Sykes who was giving up as UK representative of the Explorers' Club of New York. Egerton Sykes had himself edited and contributed to a reprint of Donnelly's *Atlantis – the Antediluvian World* and when I met him at Brighton where he lived he had one piece of advice: 'If you ever wish to get a grant to study Atlantis in Bolivia' he said, 'Then don't mention Atlantis – you can say you are going to study anything you like as long as you don't say it's Atlantis.'

That proved to be sound advice, although of course I never followed it, since my purpose was not only to study Atlantis but to bring about the recognition that the Altiplano was the site of Atlantis.

It had been Professor Raymond Dart who had recommended me to Egerton Sykes and the Explorer's Club. I met him at his hotel in London on one of his stopovers from America to Johannesburg. He was of advanced years at the time and asked me to read him a piece from the journal of the Explorer's Club. Then turning towards the window he said 'You see all those people down there,' pointing to the throngs of people ambling along Oxford Street, 'I doubt if any one of them can understand your idea.'

In those days I had the privilege of being rejected by all the noteworthies you could think of, starting with Professor Glyn Daniel who wrote me a letter calling my idea, 'The lunatic fringe of archaeology' but then I discovered he called anything he didn't like 'The lunatic fringe of archaeology'. So his reply was neither as entertaining nor original as it at first seemed. But perhaps it was enough to prevent me getting published.

I submitted papers to various Universities 'In the manner of a thesis' only to be told 'We don't accept unsolicited theses' or 'Thanks for your work which we have deposited in the college library.'

The head of a Cambridge college, also a leading archaeologist, was to reply, 'Atlantis is a subject in which I have never been interested', material returned.

When I asked opinions of the canal I had found, replies were usually favourable. When I mentioned Atlantis, there was usually no reply.

I approached a TV broadcasting company to make a film. They expressed an interest and recommended a TV production company. Eventually the TV production company made a film which, at the time of writing, I have never seen, using my idea so they said only 'as a starting point'. Then, whilst talking to me and telling me how difficult it was to raise funds, they flew an American professor deliberately to a wrong but more accessible site which, of course, was not the location of Atlantis.

All this immediately preceded the time when I was visiting the canal myself, and my objective in locating the canal on site was merely to prove that it existed so that it could subsequently be investigated by appropriate scientists.

At this time Colonel John Blashford-Snell was still interested in the project. I had been reintroduced to him having run into his Special Projects Officer in Cambridge, but JBS's (as he liked to be known) expeditions took years in the planning.

After locating the canal on site I decided to return to England since, in my view, an unpublished discovery was of little value. I sent copies of the ground and air photos of the canal to some leading archaeologists but never heard from them. My articles about the canal and Atlantis were equally rejected by all the leading newspapers and periodicals until a year and a half later it was finally accepted and published in the Royal Geographical Society's magazine, *The Geographical Magazine*.

The train pulled into Cambridge station and there was Frank, JBS's expedition officer with a bunch of flowers in his hand.

'How nice of you to meet me,' I said 'But you didn't need to go to all that trouble', pointing to the flowers, 'And how did you know I was coming?'

'I didn't,' he growled, 'And these are for my girlfriend; she'll be coming off the train at any moment. And, by the way, have you rung JBS – he's dying to hear from you?'

No I hadn't rung JBS, in fact I had had no intention since in his last letter after all the trouble I had gone to locate the canal on site, he had mentioned the dreaded 'fault lines'.

But I did ring him, acting on Frank's advice and indeed he was glad to hear from me.

So began a frequent exchange of communications and I learnt that his expedition was to be called the Kota Mama (Mother of the Lake) expedition with the purpose of sailing three traditional reed boats along the Desaguadero River from Lake Titicaca to Lake Poopo, investigating archaeological sites along the valley route, checking out my canal and looking for any other clues relative to the site of Atlantis.

The phone rang one afternoon and he asked if I had any ideas which might make the project more attractive to a film company. Bearing in mind King Solomon's fleet which could have sailed to a Tarshish in South America, I said: 'Why don't you start at the islands of the Sun and Moon in Lake Titicaca, sail your reed boats down the Desaguadero to Lake Poopo, investigate the canal, continue up to the silver mines at Mount Potosi, overland via the Tarija valley with its fossil relics and painter's landscape to the headwaters of the Pilcomayo River. Then proceed down this river which used to be called the River of Silver to the estuary at Buenos Aires, looking for the site of Tarshish on the way. Join up with a ship to cross the Atlantic, under the Cape of Good Hope via the Indian Ocean islands to Ceylon, then via the Red Sea to the Gulf of Aqaba finally proceeding on horseback overland via the city of Petra to a reconstructed court of King Solomon in Israel.'

'Mm,' he said, 'Can you write it up for me?'

A few months later the Kota Mama expedition was announced at the Boat Show in Southampton. It had acquired two extra phases, down the Pilcomayo River and across the Atlantic Ocean to Cape Town.

But this book is not just for the Kota Mama expedition. It is for all those expeditions and adventurers who may follow, building up on the groundwork I have put down so that they may seek the truth of the legend for themselves, and one day bring to light the lost civilisation of *Atlantis*.

Relief model of the Altiplano.

Key to Satellite Photographs

THESE SATELLITE PICTURES show the Earth from an altitude of 500 miles.

On these infra-red pictures, the large white patches are the salt salars formed by the constant flooding and evaporation of water on the plain.

The photo-mosaic is composed of seven pictures, each covering an area of 100 × 100 nautical miles (185 × 185 kms).

The heavy line represents the outline of the plain as defined by the 13,000 ft contour.

B The breadth of the plain is given as 2,000 stades 'At its centre, reckoning upwards from the sea' and the length as 3,000 stades. From the actual physical dimensions of the plain the stade may be identified here as a unit of nominally 300 ft and the plain seen to be in the correct ratio of 2,000:3,000 'half-stades'.

C Water is seen emerging onto the Salar de Coipasa having travelled a distance of 57 miles from Lake Poopo along a possible former canal. Compare to 'S', taken at a later date, where the water has been held back by the straight edges of former canals.

L The length of the plain is 3,000 stades, see 'B'.

S Shows the Salar de Coipasa now flooded where the water has fallen into the straight lines of former canals.

V Volcanoes of similar size to the city complex exist on the plain.

W Water is seen in a section of perimeter canal extending through X–Y.

136

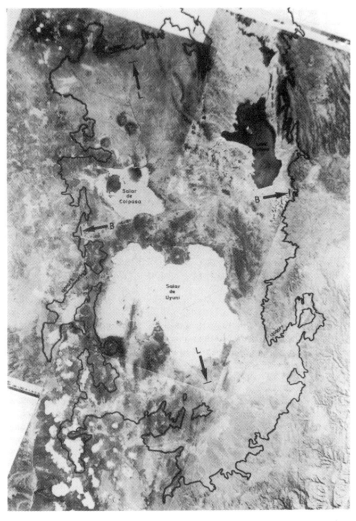

Photo mosaic of the plain. The heavy line denotes the 13,000 ft contour.

Detail of Lake Poopo, Salar de Coipasa and Salar de Uyuni. The Salar de Uyuni is 68 miles wide, with an area of 3,500 square miles.

Detail of Salar de Coipasa. In October, water is seen emerging down an old canal (C) from Lake Poopo (top right, opposite page)

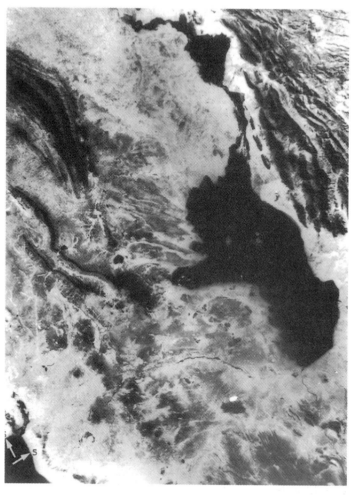

Lake Poopo, centre right. Note the right-angled straight edges at 'S', suggesting water held back by former canals.

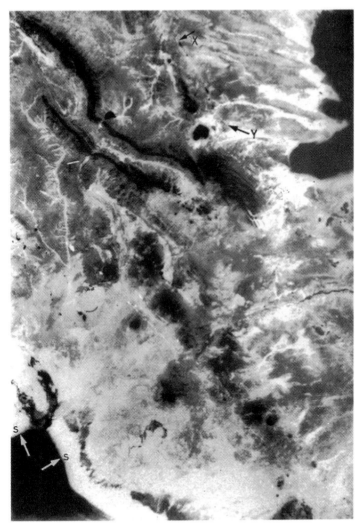

In May the Salar is flooded and the straight sections 'S' suggest the waters are held back by sections of old canals.

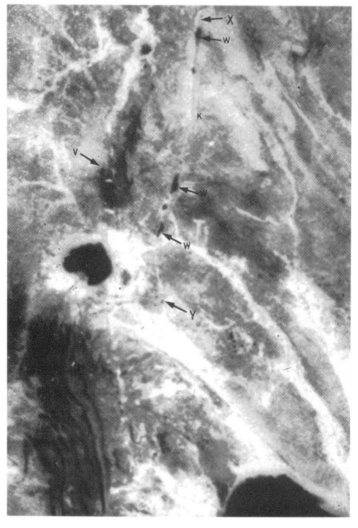

Enlargement of possible perimeter canal X–Y, showing water (W) trapped in canal sections.

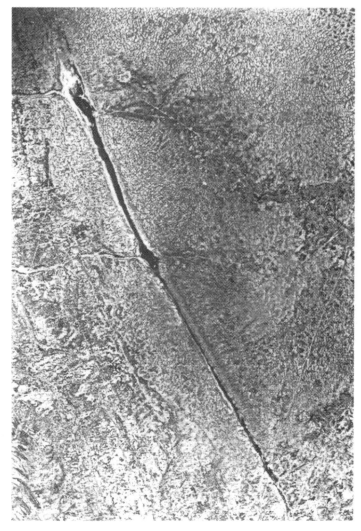

Aerial photograph of northern section of canal, X–K opposite.

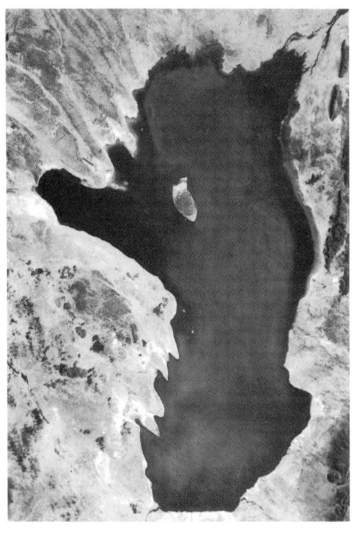

Lake Poopo, 50 miles long, the shallow sea . . . 'blocked up by the shoal mud which the island created as it settled down'.

Abandoned patchwork irrigation plots north-west of Lake Poopo.

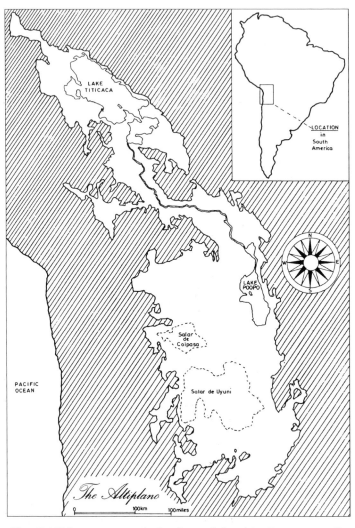

The 13,000 ft contour reveals the shape of the plain. 'It was originally a quadrangle, rectilinear for the most part, and elongated.'

South America.

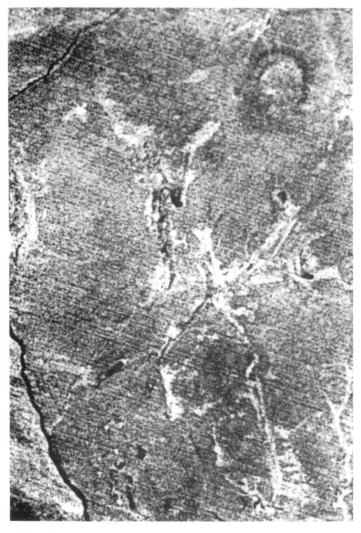

Greatly enlarged image showing large-scale canalisation leading to circular volcanic caldera.

Last Thoughts

SHOULD THERE BE any inconsistencies in Plato's story, we must remember the story was successively retold over the generations in addition to being translated first from the Atlantean tongue into Egyptian, then into Greek and finally into English.

The shallow sea of Lake Poopo has not always had the shape and form it has today, it changes location and varies in area according to the amount of water and climatic changes.

The perimeter canal is presented as a regular rectangular grid in some translations whereas Plato merely says the canals were cut across the plain at regular intervals and connected by transverse passages – these could equally well be diagonal as well as vertical. Other translations merely say the perimeter canal *made the circuit* of the plain, or as Donnelly put it, it *wound round* the plain, suggesting that up to a point, it followed the natural contours of the plain taking into account natural volcanic outcrops etc.

Greatly enlarged imagery of the north centre of the plain shows clear evidence of large scale canalisation – leading to what appears at first glance to be a spiral ring but closer inspection suggests concentric or eccentric circles – the outer ring three stades wide at its widest and approached by a canal fifty stades long which could correspond to the one which Plato says led in the very beginning to the sea.

The location fits the translation by Lee, that the original mountain was near the middle of the plain about fifty stades inland,[2] i.e. it is 50 stades from the centre of the plain measured not lengthwise along the plain as in the 'classical' view presented by Bury and Lee, but 50 stades from the centre of the plain measured across the width of the plain as Plato described it 'reckoning upwards from the sea'.[1]

The overall width of the feature corresponds to 27 stades or three statute miles which is the width Plato quoted for the centre complex and a navigation chart shows a volcanic horseshoe-shaped ring rising 500 ft above the level plain.

Could this be the original 'low mountain' as Plato called it, which became the site of the sought after city? Or merely a similarity on this Mysterious Altiplano? As one scientist put it regarding the canals, 'Ground inspection is the only answer!'

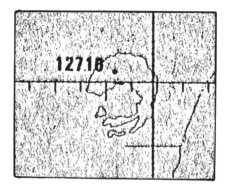

Atlantis

Plato's statements relative to the Altiplano

1 The whole country was of continental size.

2 It was opposite the Pillars of Hercules.

3 In the centre of the continent there was a plain.

4 The plain was next to the sea.

5 The plain was an elongated rectangle.

6 The plain was enclosed by mountains.

7 The plain had a level surface.

8 The plain was high above the ocean sea.

9 The plain contains volcanoes of similar size to that upon which the city was built.

10 The plain was midway along the longest side of the continent.

11 The plain had a system of canals.

12 The region faced south, as seen on the Inca map.

13 Hot and cold springs exist on the plain.

14 The plain is prone to earthquakes.

15 The plain is prone to floods.

16 The region rises sheer out of the sea on this side of the continent.

151

17 The surrounding mountains contained lakes and streams.

18 The mountains contained gold.

19 The mountains contained silver.

20 The mountains contained copper.

21 The mountains contained tin.

22 The mountains contained a natural alloy of copper and gold.

23 Temples were hung in gold sheets as was the custom amongst later Incas.

24 Statues in gold was also a custom amongst the Incas.

25 The first inhabitants were born in pairs.

26 Natives of the plain speak a dialect similar to North-African berber.

27 Elephant-like mastodons existed in South America.

28 The plain was flooded around 9,000 BC.

29 A lunar calendar brings the date of the war to 1263 BC i.e. the date of the Trojan War.

30 A lunar calendar existed on Crete.

31 A lunar calendar existed amongst the Inca.

32 Confederated nations attacked Greece and Egypt following on from the Trojan War.

33 The attacking Sea Peoples wore feathered head-dresses.

34 South American cocaine has been found in ancient Egypt.

35 A flood legend exists on the Altiplano.

36 In the Aztec language 'atl' means 'water'.

37 In Peruvian Quechua 'antis' means 'copper'.

38 Antis is the correct name for the Andes mountains.

39 The Inca called part of their empire Antisuyo.

40 The Aztecs claimed to have come from 'Aztlan'.

41 The Aztecs built a fortified city similar to Atl-Antis.

42 The Aztecs lived amongst water similar to the Uru peoples of the Altiplano whose kingdom was Uma (water) suyo.

43 The configuration of the Altiplano could support Plato's perimeter canal.

44 A section of 600 ft wide channel exists on the rectangular Altiplano.

45 Square irrigated plots exist on the Altiplano.

46 The plain measures 3,000 × 2,000 'stades' of 300 ft.

47 The city had to be on an inland sea because the whole region was high above the level of the ocean.

48 Beyond Atlantis (South America) there lay islands (in the Pacific) which led to a continent (Asia).

49 A legend of a golden city by a lake (El Dorado) exists in South America.

50 The sea in those parts (Lake Poopo) was unsearchable due to the shoal mud.

Plato's Statements and a Commentary

1 **Time – Atlantis, 9,000 years before Solon.**
The Altiplano was indeed flooded at this time but the '9,000 years' also referred to the founding of Athens and a period of wars. If the 9,000 'years' were in fact 9,000 months, this could refer to the creation of the state of Athens by Theseus who also freed the Greeks from the labyrinth and saved the Greeks from Cretan domination (1400 BC). The Greek invasion of Troy in 1260 BC could correspond to 'the noblest of the deeds they performed' and the wars continued with the subsequent invasion of Egypt by the Sea Peoples in 1220 and 1186 BC.

2 **'In front of the Pillars of Hercules, there lay an island which was larger than Libya and Asia together.'**
The continents of North and South America lie directly in front of the Pillars of Hercules (Strait of Gibraltar) and could be considered an island in the midst of the great world-circling Ocean. Disregarding the narrow Panama isthmus, South America could easily be described as an island in its own right. It is almost totally surrounded by water and lies substantially to the east of the northern continent. Its land surface occupies 14 per cent of the world's land area although by 'Libya and Asia together', only the then known inhabited regions were probably intended, i.e. what we would now call North Africa and the Middle East. Probably South America rather than the whole of the Americas is specifically intended since it has the plain at its centre, midway along its longest side etc and it had the original pre-conquest Inca name of Tahuantisuyo.

3 **'Starting from a distant point in the Atlantic Ocean.'**
South America may be regarded as a distant point in the Atlantic Ocean and the Altiplano more so, particularly since the river route to the Atlantic involves some 1500 miles of inland waterways.

4 'It was possible for the travellers of that time to cross from it to the other islands, and from the islands to the whole of the continent over against them which encompasses that veritable ocean.'

The crossing here is from Europe/Africa to Atlantis (South America) and thence via the various Pacific islands to continental Asia.

5 'All we have here within the mouth is evidently a haven having a narrow entrance.'

Valid statement confirming Plato's own ignorance of world geography since use of the word 'evidently' suggests he is indeed handing on the story as he heard it.

6 'That yonder is a real ocean and the land surrounding it may be most rightly called, in the fullest and truest sense, a continent.'

The real ocean is the Atlantic/Pacific containing the 'island' of Atlantis (South America) and the continental land surrounding it is that of Africa/Europe/Asia.

7 'At a later time there occurred portentous earthquakes and floods and one grievous day and night . . . the island of Atlantis was swallowed up by the sea and vanished.' (Bury). 'In a single day and night *of rain* . . . the island of Atlantis disappeared.' (Donnelly).

The island here referred to is the island capital or Royal City, sometimes called the Ancient Metropolis, built on a volcanic caldera forming an island in a huge inland sea or lake. This lake, (Lake Poopo), was next to the irrigated plain and served it as a reservoir. Note the end came in a single day and night of *rain*. The entire level plain could be easily flooded in a period of torrential rain with possibly violent reactions from active volcanoes and the ejection of lava, volcanic ash or poisonous gases could further have rendered large areas of the country uninhabitable.

8 'The ocean at that spot has now become impassable and unsearchable, being blocked up by the shoal mud which the island created as it settled down.'

Lake Poopo is indeed choked up and has a depth of only ten to fifteen feet. It is fifty miles long and entirely filled with salt water. In the wet season some of this water spills onto the plain eventually to evaporate leaving widespread deposits of salt.

9 'Those Egyptians who had first written the record down had translated it into their own tongue . . . Solon recovered the

original sense of each name and, rendering it into our tongue (Greek) wrote it down so.'
Solon preserved the correct numbers but gave the units Greek names, some of which had double the value of the originals.

10 **'Poseidon took for his allotment the island of Atlantis and settled therein the children whom he had begotten of a mortal woman in a region of the island of the following description.'**
The 'island' is South America.

11 **'Bordering on the sea and extending through the centre of the whole island there was a plain.'**
The sea may be either the inland sea of Lake Titicaca (called Titicaca Sea locally)/Lake Poopo (also called Poopo Sea) or the Pacific Ocean. Extending through the centre of the Andean mountain range which is itself next to the Ocean Sea, is a plain, the Bolivian Plateau or Altiplano. It is exactly in the centre of the longest side of the continent and it is remarkable that the translation by Desmond Lee adds the precise footnote 'i.e. midway along its greatest length'.

12 **'Which was said to be the fairest of all plains and highly fertile.'**
The plain is surrounded by volcanic mountains; volcanic ash forms the most fertile soil in the world.

13 **'Near its centre at a distance of about fifty stades there stood a mountain that was low on all sides.'**
The site of the mountain was to become the site of the city and its location is important. The plain 'extending through the centre of the whole island' includes Lake Titicaca in the north and reaches as far as the Cordillera de Lipez in the south with Lake Poopo near its centre. But within the overall plateau we have the rectangular plain adjacent to Lake Poopo and it seems that the city lay near the centre of the plain, at a distance of fifty stades (five miles) from the sea.

14 **'To make it fully impregnable he broke it off all round about; and he made circular belts of sea and land enclosing one another alternately, some greater, some smaller, two being of land and three of sea.'**
Describes the utilisation of a volcanic caldera of similar size to the numerous other volcanic cones dotted about the plain. The natural volcanic rings formed perfect natural harbours and the flooding of the adjacent plain due to, say, the diversion of local rivers would create an admirable island fortress.

15 'For, beginning at the sea, they bored a channel right through
   to the outermost circle which was fifty stades in length; and
   thus they made an entrance to it from the sea like that to a
   harbour by opening out a mouth large enough for the greatest
   ships to sail through.'
   The location of the natural harbours was fifty stades from the sea
   (lake) as this was the length of canal required to give access to the
   sea.

16 'And after crossing the three outer harbours, one found a wall
   which began at the sea and ran round in a circle, at a uniform
   distance of fifty stades from the largest circle and harbour.'
   The creation of the sea wall gave extra land to the city and prevented
   the location from flooding.

17 'And he begat five pairs of twin sons and reared them up, and
   when he had divided all the island of Atlantis into ten portions,
   he assigned to the first-born of the eldest sons his mother's
   dwelling and the allotment surrounding it, which was the largest and the best; him he appointed to be king over the rest,
   and the others to be rulers, granting to each the rule over many
   men and a large tract of country.'
   Inca legend tells that the first inhabitants were born in pairs.

18 'And to all of them he gave names, giving to him that was the
   eldest and king the name after which the whole island was
   called and the sea spoken of as the Atlantic, because the first
   king who then reigned had the name of Atlas.'
   Atlas came to be associated with the mountain range of that name
   in West Africa. The true mountains of Atlans are those of the Andean
   chain.[39]

19 'And the name of his younger twin-brother, who had for his
   portion the extremity of the island near the Pillars of Hercules
   . . . was in the native tongue Gadeirus.'
   The Pillars of Hercules was the general name for the Strait of Gibraltar
   and usually identified with Mt Calpe on the European side of the
   Strait and Mt Abyle on the African side; it is sometimes said they
   were originally called 'the Pillars of Cronus'.[39]
   The king of Tyre sent out an expedition to found a colony near the
   Pillars of Hercules and the site chosen was Gades (modern Cadiz).
   A temple was erected in honour of Hercules with brazen columns
   eight cubits high which also became known as 'the Pillars of Hercules'.

20 **'The island furnished most of the requirements of daily life.'**
South America is a country of tremendous natural resources.

21 **'Metals to begin with, both of the hard kind and the fusible kind, which are extracted by mining.'**
The country and Bolivia in particular is rich in metals including gold, silver, copper, tin, iron, lead, zinc, antimony, wolfram and natural alloys.

22 **'And also that kind which is now known only by name but was more than a name then – I mean orichalcum, which was the most precious of the metals then known, except gold.'**
Orichalcum was probably a naturally occurring alloy involving copper. Bury considered it to be 'mountain copper' – 'a sparkling metal hard to identify'. Lee considered it to be a 'completely unknown and imaginary metal,' i.e. an invention of Plato. Bronze is a mixture of copper and tin and brass an alloy of copper and zinc. But a more 'sparkling' and valuable metal was known to the Inca – a gleaming alloy of copper and gold which occurs naturally only in the Andes.

23 **'It brought forth also in abundance all the timbers that a forest provides for the use of carpenters.'**
The Amazonian jungles are the largest afforested areas in the world.

24 **'And of animals it produced a sufficiency, both of tame and of wild.'**
South America is home to a multitude of species, well known for its ferocious wild beasts and also for the Andean herds of llama and alpaca – valuable for the production of fine wool.

25 **'Moreover it contained a very large stock of elephants.'**
At a depth of 17 ft in Veracruz, the remains of human occupation were found – Indian hunters from 5,600 BC; also the remains of a mastodon (a primitive, swamp loving type of elephant). Mastodons previously ranged over North and South America and were thought to have become extinct around 6000 BC although some Mayan carvings from a much later period depict elephant-like features.

26 **'For there was an ample food supply not only for all the other animals which haunt the marshes and lakes and rivers, or the mountains or the plains.'**
South America is a land of marshes, lakes, rivers, mountains and plains.

27 'In addition it produced and brought to perfection all those sweet scented stuffs which the earth produces now, whether made of roots or herbs or trees, or of liquid gums derived from fruits.'

South America produces all these and is the home of the liquid gum or rubber tree.

28 'The cultivated fruit also, and the dry, which serves us for nutriment, and all the other kinds comprehended under the name vegetable.'

Many of our modern foods from tomatoes to maize or corn originated in the Americas. The Altiplano is the natural home of the potato and 150 varieties may be found there.

29 'And all the produce of trees which affords liquid and solid food and unguents, and the fruit of the orchard trees, and all the after-dinner fruits that we serve up as welcome remedies for the sufferer from repletion.'

Practically any fruit or crop could be grown in some region of South America. Many plants were first domesticated here and selective husbandry of particular strains improved the crops over successive generations.

30 'First of all they bridged over the circles of sea which surrounded the ancient metropolis. Now the island and the circles and the bridge, they encompassed round about with a wall of stone . . . some of it being white, some black and some red.'

Black and red stone is typical of a volcanic region, also of the Altiplano.

31 'And they covered with brass all the circumference of the wall which surrounded the outermost circle.'

Brass is an alloy of copper and zinc. Deposits of copper and zinc must occur near the city.

32 'And that of the inner one they coated with tin.'

Major deposits of tin must occur near the city.

33 'And that which encompassed the acropolis itself with orichalcum which sparkled like fire.' (Bury) or 'Flashed with the red light of orichalcum.' (Donnelly).

Major deposits of orichalcum (copper/gold alloy) must occur near the city.

34 'In the centre there stood a temple encircled with a wall of gold.'
Major deposits of gold must occur near the city.

35 'All the exterior of the temple they coated with silver, save only
the pinnacles, and these they coated with gold.'
Major deposits of silver must occur near the city.

36 'They made the roof all of ivory in appearance, variegated with
gold and silver and orichalcum.'
All these metals may be found in the region of Lake Poopo. Eighty
per cent of Bolivia's vast mineral deposits occur in the Cordilleria
Real, a section of the Eastern Andes running from the Peruvian
border, south through Bolivia to the Argentine border, with gold
deposits in the north, copper along the Eastern Altiplano and deposits of silver and tin in the region from Oruro to Potosi.[45] The
legendary Potosi with its mountain of silver, and tin mines, lies only
eighty miles from the lake as does the Cochambamba Valley with a
host of non-ferrous metals. The region around and east of Lake
Poopo is where all the valuable seams come together. Gold and
copper mines exist which are still worked to this day including
Corocoro and Oruro which is the modern centre of the mining
industry. Many mines produce more than one metal and sometimes
as many as four metals are found occurring naturally together. An
ancient city on or near the lake would also have been a natural
centre for a metals industry with so many valuable deposits at hand.

37 'And they placed therein golden statues, one being that of the
God standing on a chariot and driving six winged steeds, his
own figure so tall as to touch the ridge of the roof, and round
about him a hundred Nereids on dolphins. And outside, there
stood images in gold of all the princes, both themselves and
their wives, as many as were descended from the ten kings.'
The later Inca continued the custom of making life-sized golden
statues of their ancestors.

38 'And the wealth they possessed was so immense that the like
had never been seen before in any royal house nor will ever
be easily seen again.'
The closest thing to approach it was the wealth of the Inca, who
had temples hung with gold sheets and completely filled a store
room 20 ft × 17 ft with golden objects as ransom to the avaricious
Pizarro.

39 'The springs they made use of, one kind being of cold, another
of warm water . . . they put separate baths for the kings and

for the private citizens, besides others for women.'
Hot and cold springs occur on the Altiplano and baths with hot and cold water piped from natural sources were also constructed by the Inca.

40 **'In the first place then, according to the account the whole region rose sheer out of the sea to a great height.' (Bury).**
It is important to realise that the plain was high above the level of the sea. Lee, 'To begin with the region as a whole was said to be high above the level of the sea, from which it rose precipitously.' The region rises sheer out of the sea (the Pacific) to a height of 20,000 ft for the mountains and 12,000 ft for the tableland or plain.

41 **'But the part about the city was all a smooth plain, enclosing it round about, and being itself encircled by mountains which stretched as far as to the sea.'**
The part about Lake Poopo is a smooth plain, enclosing it round about, and being itself encircled by mountains which stretch as far as the sea (the Pacific). Note the plain was enclosed by mountains *on all sides* – Lee, 'The city was surrounded by a uniformly flat plain which was in turn *enclosed by mountains.*'

42 **'And this plain had a level surface.'**
The plain is remarkably flat, 11,985 ft above sea level at both the Salar de Coipasa and Salar de Uyuni and constitutes the largest level area in the world.

43 **'And was as a whole rectangular in shape, being 3,000 stades long on either side and 2,000 stades wide at its centre, reckoning upwards from the sea.'**
The smooth and level plain around the city is enclosed by surrounding mountains to form a quadrangular basin within the elongated plain known as the Bolivian Plateau. It is, as Plato correctly reports, of rectangular configuration – 3,000 stades long on either side and 2,000 stades wide at its centre, reckoning upwards from the sea, Lake Poopo. The stade here is an original unit of 300 ft, i.e. half a Greek stadium.

44 **'And this region all along the island, faced towards the South.'**
The plain is on the side of the continent nearest the south Sea or Southern Ocean. What we now call the Atlantic was then called 'The Sea of the North'.

45 **'The condition of the plain was this; it was originally a quad-rangle, rectilinear for the most part, and elongated; and what**

it lacked of this shape they made right by means of a trench dug round about it.'

It would be impossible to improve on Bury's rendering of the plain as being 'a quadrangle, rectilinear and elongated'. Lee tells us 'It was naturally a long, regular rectangle.' Both perfect descriptions of the section of plain adjacent to Lake Poopo and surely unique in the world especially when combined with all the other factors. The primary purpose of the trench was to form the basis of an irrigation scheme.

46 '**Now as regards the depth of this trench and its breadth and length, it seems incredible that it should be so large as the account states . . . it was dug out to a depth of a plethrum and to a uniform breadth of a stade, and since it was dug round the whole of the plain its consequent length was 10,000 stades**.'

A plethrum was a Greek unit of 100 ft but we must assume the depth was 100 Atlantean units – possibly 50 ft. The breadth of the channel as has been confirmed by the site visit was a 'stade' of 600 ft. The length of the perimeter trench was 10,000 'half-stades' of 300 ft which can be confirmed from the length of the plain. The digging of this and the cross trenches is no mean achievement but it should be borne in mind that these trenches would be of 'V' shaped profile, thus reducing the amount of ground removed, also that the soil consisted of soft, sandy material.

47 '**It received the streams which came down from the mountains and after circling round the plain, and coming towards the city on this side and on that, it discharged them thereabouts into the sea**.'

Again the Altiplano is unique in that the smooth and level plain is surrounded by mountains with numerous lakes and streams which drain onto the plain. By digging a ditch around the perimeter of the plain, the waters from the mountains could indeed be collected and discharged into Lake Poopo which would act as a kind of reservoir.

48 '**And on the inland side of the city channels were cut in straight lines, of about 100 ft in width, across the plain, and these discharged themselves into the trench on the seaward side, the distance between each being 100 stades**.'

The channels and cross channels completed the irrigation scheme by draining into the major trench on the far perimeter of the plain. The perimeter trench was larger than the other trenches not primarily to accommodate plying craft but to facilitate the flow of water to and from the reservoir (Lake Poopo) and the smaller trenches.

49 'It was in this way that they conveyed to the city the timber from the mountains and transported also on boats the seasons' products, by cutting transverse passages from one channel to the next, and also to the city.'

The trenches served additionally as a canalised transportation system.

50 'And they cropped the land twice a year, making use of the rains from Heaven in the winter, and the waters that issue from the earth in summer, by conducting the streams from the trenches.'

In the wet season, the canals drained off the surplus waters to other areas. In the dry season, the water flowed to the plain from Lake Poopo, supplemented by the much larger Lake Titicaca. The canalised trench system thus provided both drainage and irrigation and brought fertility to the land throughout the year.

Source Books

NB. The number before each reference refers to superscript figures in the text

1 Bury, R. G., Plato IX *Timaeus, Critias* etc., Harvard University Press, 1929
2 Lee, Desmond, Plato *Timaeus* and *Critias*, Penguin Books, 1965
3 Dilke, Christopher, *Letter to a King*, George Allen & Unwin
4 Hancock, Ralph, *Mexico*, Macmillan
5 Von Hagen, Victor W., *Realm of the Incas*
6 Carter, William, *Bolivia – A Profile*, Praeger Publishers, 1971
7 Larco Hoyle, Rafael, *The Ancient Civilisation of Peru*, Barrie & Jenkins, 1967
8 *Fodor's Guide to South America 1979*, Fodors, 1979
9 Honore, Pierre, *In Quest of the White God*, Hutchinson
10 *Ancient America*, Time Life Books
11 *Living Architecture – Mayan*, Oldebury Book Co., 1964
12 Kendall, Ann, *Everyday Life of the Incas*, B. T. Batsford Ltd, 1973
13 Slesser, Malcolm, *Discovery of South America*, Hamlyn, 1970
14 Savoy, Gene, *Vilcabamba – Last City of the Incas*, Robert Hale
15 Fawcett, Lt. Col. P. H., *Exploration Fawcett*, The Companion Book Club, 1954
16 Donnelly, Ignatius, *Atlantis the ante-diluvian world*, Harper & Bros, NY, 1882
17 Mavor, J. W., *Voyage to Atlantis*, Fontana, 1969
18 Braghine, Col. A., *The Shadow of Atlantis*, The Aquarian Press Ltd, 1940/ 1980
19 Sprague de Camp, L., *Lost Continents*, Dover, 1970
20 Alsop, Joseph, *From the Silent Earth*, Secker & Warburg, 1965
21 Cotterell, Leonard, *The Bull of Minos*, Evans Bros Ltd, 1962
22 Quenell, Marjorie & C. H. B., *Everyday Things in Ancient Greece*, B. T. Batsford Ltd, 1954
23 Saunders, N. K., *The Sea Peoples*, Thames & Hudson, 1985
24 *Larousse Mythology*, Larousse, 1959
25 *Mythology of the Americas*, Hamlyn, 1970
26 *Evolution*, Time Life, 1970

27 Claiborne, Robert, *Climate, Man and History*, Angus & Robertson, 1973

28 John, Brian S., *The Ice Age Past & Present*, Collins, 1977

29 Leakey, Richard E., *Origins*, Macdonald & Janes, 1977

30 Magnusson, Magnus, BC *The Archaeology of the Bible Lands*, Bodley Head, 1977

31 Berriman, A. E., *Historical Metrology*, J. M. Dent & Sons Ltd, 1953

32 Thom, A., *Megalithic Sites in Britain*, Clarendon Press, 1967

33 Thompkins, Peter, *Secrets of the Great Pyramid*, Penguin Books, 1973

34 Hapgood, Charles, *Maps of the Ancient Sea Kings*, Turnstone Books, 1966

35 Hapgood, Charles, *The Path of the Pole*, Turnstone Books

36 Evans, Humphrey, *The Mystery of the Pyramids*, Marshall Cavendish, 1979

37 Pendlebury, John, *The Archaeology of Crete*, Methuen, 1965

38 Marcus, Joyce, *Zapotec Writing*, Scientific American, February 1980

39 Graves, Robert, *The Greek Myths*, Penguin, 1955

40 Swaney, Deanna, *Bolivia – a travel survival kit*, Lonely Planet, 1988

41 Verrill, Hyatt and Ruth, *America's Ancient Civilisations*, G. P. Putnam's Sons N.Y., 1954

42 Coe, Michael D., *Mexico*, Thames & Hudson, 1984

43 Davies, Nigel, *The Aztecs*, Macmillan, 1977

44 Hemming, John, *The Search for El Dorado*, Michael Joseph, 1978

45 Klein, Herbert S., *Bolivia*, Oxford University Press, 1992

46 Aveni, Anthony, *Empires of Time*, I. B. Taurus & Co. Ltd, 1990

47 Cornell, James, *The First Stargazers*, The Athlone Press, 1981

48 Ward, A. G., *The Quest for Theseus*, Pall Mall Press, 1990

49 Anthony, Michael, *The Golden Quest*, Macmillan, 1992

50 Prescott, William H., *The Conquest of Peru*, Harper N.Y.C., 1847

51 Blavatsky, H. P., *Isis Unveiled*, Theosophical Publishing House, 1877

52 Fasold, David, *The Discovery of Noah's Ark*, David Fasold, Sidgwick & Jackson, 1990

53 Heyerdahl, Thor, *The Tigris Expedition*, Doubleday & Co., 1982

54 Howse, Derek, *Greenwich Time and the Discovery of Longitude*, Oxford University Press, 1980

55 Castlereagh, Duncan, *The Great Age of Exploration*, Readers Digest/Aldus Books, 1971

56 Harden, Donald, *The Phoenicians*, Pelican Books, 1980

57 Bacon, Francis, *The New Atlantis*, Cambridge University Press, 1900 (Original edition 1627)

58 Childress David Hatcher, *Lost Cities and Ancient Mysteries of South America*, Adventures Unlimited Press, 1985

59 *Guide to Peru*, Ediciones de Arte Rep, Lima

Acknowledgements

The publishers would like to thank the following for the use of extracts and illustrations. All efforts have been made to trace the copyright holders but the publishers would be happy to hear from anyone they have not been able to trace. The translated extracts from Plato and the illustration on page 49 are reprinted by the permission of the publishers and the Loeb Classical Library from PLATO: VOL IX translated by R. G. Bury, Cambridge, Mass.: Harvard University Press, 1929; pages v, 91, 100 and 147 courtesy of David Hatcher Childress, *Lost Cities and Ancient Mysteries of South America*, Adventures Unlimited Press; pages 14, 56 and 58 courtesy of Ignatius Donnelly's *Atlantis*; page 3 courtesy of the British Museum; page 66 by courtesy of Oriental Institute, University of Chicago; page 67 courtesy of the Ashmolean Museum, Oxford; page 89 from *Image of the New World* by Gordon Brotherston published by Thames & Hudson Ltd; page 76 from *The Great Temple of the Aztecs* by Eduardo Matos Moctezuma, published by Thames & Hudson Ltd; page 87 Time Life Ltd; page 1, colour section, courtesy of Reader's Digest Association Ltd; page 3 (lower) colour section 2 courtesy of Lonely Planet Publications.

Index

Abyle, Mt., 157
Acre, 92
Acropolis, of Athens; 37–38; of
    Atlantis, 42–44
Acte, Istmus of, 104
Aerial Photos, 122–126, 143, 145
Africa, 54, 81, 106, 112, 117
Al Mamun, Caliph, 111
Alphabet, 52
Altiplano, 1, 4–6, 10, 13, 15, 18,
    22–28, 61, 78, 81–82, 104, 130;
    cross section, 22, 27; map of,
    23, 146; climate of, 81, 82;
    relief model, 135
Allotments, 39, 40, 45
Alloy, 21, 96–97, 99, 158
Altitude, 121, 127
Alto Peru, 1
Amadis, legend of, 78
Amasis, King, 30
Amazonia, 4
Amazon, River, 51, 84, 94
Amazons, 83–84
America, 5, 15, 52–57, 115;
    central, 52, 54, 73, 75, 95; early
    civilisation, 71; north, 81–82;
    origin of name, 2; south, 1–6,
    15, 19, 51, 74, 81–82, 115, 120;
    south, map of, 147
Amphora, 68–69
Amynander, 30

Andamarea, 128
Andes, 1, 4, 11, 86, 88, 99, 103,
    152; metals of, 96; tunnels of,
    98–100
Antarctica, 116
Antilles, 4
Antillia, 3–4
Antimony, 21
Antis, 4, 10, 152; map, 90
Antisuyo, 4, 10; map, 88–90
Apaturia, 30
Aqaba, Gulf of, 134
Aqueducts, 56–57, 79
Ararat, Mt., 117–118
Ark, 53, 56, 117–118
Aryan, 52
Asia, 9, 15, 33–34, 38, 54, 60
Asunción, 104
Atacama Desert, 99
Atahualpa, 1, 98–99
Athena, 31–32, 34–35, 61; temple
    of, 38
Athens, 29, 35, 61–62, 67–68, 82;
    founding of, 61, 154;
    confederacy of, 82
Athenians, 38, 53, 65
Atl, 4
Atlatl, 74
Atlan, city of, 75
Atlanta, 4
Atlantic Ocean, 9, 11, 33, 51–54,

60–61, 106, 112, 117, 133–134, 154–155
Atlantis, 1, 4, 5, 18–19, 22, 25, 33–35, 51–54, 58–61, 102, 111, 119, 122, 134; army of, 29; date of, 37, 61–63, 67–68, 154; docks of, 42; circles of, 41–44; city of, *see* 'city'; confederation of, 19, 33; cross of, 42; empire of, 13, 104, 116; explanation of name, 10; fleet of, 65; harbours of, 44; history of, 9, 13; island of, 39, 40, 42; founding of, 13; illustration, 46; kings of, 4, 12, 35, 40–43, 47, 62; legend in Egypt, 82; map of, 16–17; metropolis of, 41–42, 60, 63, 155, 159; palaces of, 41–42; plain of, *see* 'plain'; religion of, 52; source of, 29; swallowed by sea, 34; temples of, 42, 47
Atlas, Mt., 4; King, 18, 40, 48
Aymara, 83, 96
Aztec, 4, 10, 73–79, 123, 153; canals, 72
Aztlan, 73, 76

Babylon, 94
Bacon, Sir Francis, 52–54
Baetis, River, 103
Barleycorn, 93
Bering Strait, 109
Blashford-Snell, Col John, 128, 131–132
Bolivar, Simon, 1
Bolivia, 1, 21, 57–58, 99, 112, 121
Brass, 21, 42, 97, 103; composition of, 96, 159
Brazil, 81, 106, 120
Bronze, 97, 116; composition of, 57–58, 96
Bronze Age, 52, 68
Buenos Aires, 102, 104, 133

Bulls, on Atlantis, 47, 62; on Crete, 63–64
Byblos, 116

Cadiz, 104–105, 157
Caesars, city of, 85
Cajamarca, 98
Calendar, 114, 152
Calpe, Mt., 157
Cambridge, 7
Canaan, 118–119
Canals, 5, 7, 12–13, 85–87, 104, 111, 122 129–130, 149, 163; illustration, 24, 46, 50, 72; in Tenochtitlan, 77–79; *see also*, 'channels', 'ditch'
Canary Islands, 107
Carthage, 110–111, 115, 119; end of, 119; founding of, 104
Carthaginians, 53, 58
Cassidy, Butch, 127
Catavi, Mt., 99
Cecrops, 36
Cerne, 83–84
Channels, 25, 41, 44, 60, 129, 162; *see also* 'canals', 'ditch', 'trench'
Charles II, 108
Chavin, 71, 93
Chile, 85, 99
China, 53, 112
Chipaya, 83
Cities, old, 119–120
City, of Atlantis, 10–12, 21, 25, 47, 77; description of, 41–44; location of, 60–61, 149–150, 156; metals of, 42, 99, 159–160
Cleito, 39, 42, 60
Coca, 113
Cocaine, 111–113
Cochabamba Valley, 160
Coipasa, cross section, 27; Salar de, 83; village of, 83

Colla, 96
Columbia, 112
Columbus, Christopher, 2, 4, 15, 107
Confederation, 152; of Athens, 82; of Atlantis, 19, 33; of Sea Peoples, 67
Conquest, the Spanish, 20, 57, 75, 78, 97
Copper, 4, 10–11, 21, 58, 97, 103, 116
Copper Age, 57
Cordilleria de Lipez, 17
Coricancha, 98, 114
Corocoro, 11,160
Cortes, 78
Crete, 59, 62, 64–65, 70, 82; labyrinth of, 67; map of, 63
Critias, 9, 29–30, 59, 61
Cronus, Pillars of, 157
Cubit, 4–5, 93–94, 118; Egyptian, 117; great, 94; royal Egyptian, 93, 111, 116; sacred, 94; Sumerian, 117
Cuneiform, 116
Cuzco, 2, 91, 97–99, 114
Cyprus, 68, 111

Daniel, Prof Glyn, 132
Darien, Isthmus of, 81
Dart, Prof Raymond, 131
Darwin, Charles, 8, 20
Deluge, *see* flood
Desaguadero, River, 133; cross section, 27; map of, 26
Deucalion, 31, 38
Dilke, Christopher, 93
Dilmun, island of, 118
Dido, Princess, 110
Donnelly, Ignatius, 6, 51–58
Diomede, islands, 109
Ditch, 60; *see also* 'canals', 'channels', 'trench',

Dorians, 65
Dropides, 30

Earth, 5, 94, 107, 111, 114
Earthquakes, 34–38, 53, 61, 65, 67, 82, 151, 155
East Cape, 109–110
Ecuador, 98, 112
Eden, Garden of, 51, 56, 94–95, 102
Egypt, 8, 13, 18, 30, 40, 52, 59, 62, 65, 82, 111–113, 116, 117; delta of, 30, 59, 65; founding of, 61; measuring units, 93; priests, 36; shipping, 53
El Dorado, 84–85, 153
Elba, island of, 110
Elephants, 19, 41, 64, 158
Elysian Fields, 51, 111; illustration, 112
Equator, 81–82
Eumelus, 18
Euphrates, River, 116, 118
Europe, 15, 33, 34, 38, 54, 57, 58, 81
Evans, Arthur, 59
Evenor, 39
Ezekiel, 5, 94, 102

Fasold, David, 117
Fault lines, 7
Fawcett, Col P.H., 119–120
Flood, 2, 12, 31, 34, 37, 52–55, 67, 76, 82, 116, 118, 151, 152; glyph, 28; *see also* 'deluge'
Foot, 92–94; origin of, 94, 111
Fortunate Isles, 107
Furlong, 92, 94

Gadeira, 18, 40, 104, 157
Gades, 104–105, 119, 157
Gê, 32
Gebel, 102

Gibraltar, Strait of, 2, 15–16, 60–61, 112
Gilgamesh, 116
Gold, 11, 21, 38, 40, 42, 48, 54, 57, 64, 96–99, 102–103, 116, 160; of the Andes, 97; river of, 104
Gomara, Francisco Lopez de, 52–53
Graves, Robert, 82
Greece, 59, 62, 104
Greeks, 34, 37, 65, 67, 68
Greenwich, 106, 108, 115
Guadalquivir, River, 102
Guara, 113
Guahani, 2
Guardians, 36, 62
Guatavita, Lake, 85

Hannibal, 119
Haiti, 2
Harbours, of Atlantis, 44, 157
Harrison, John, 115
Hebrews, 118–119
Helios, 31
Hellas, 36
Hellenes, 35
Hephaestus, 32, 35; temple of, 38
Hera, 4
Heracles, Pillars of, 18, 33–35, 40; *see also* 'Hercules'
Heraclids, 65
Hercules, Pillars of, 9, 54, 60, 61, 64, 104–105, 151, 154; explanation, 157; *see also* 'Heracles'
Hermocrates, 34
Hesiod, 30
Hesperides, 4; Gardens of, 51
Heyerdahl, Thor, 116–117
Himera, 119
Hiram, 102–103, 119
Hojeda, Alonso de, 2

Homer, 30, 54, 59, 65
Honoré, Pierre, 96
Horses, 20, 43–45, 82
Huascar, 98
Hudsons Bay, 81

Inca, 1–2, 11, 26, 78, 86, 97–99, 114–115, 153; empire, 88–90, 98; gold, 97; measurement, 92, 94; time, 114–115
Inch, 111
Indian Ocean, 113, 133
Indo-European, 52
Indus, 93
Indus Valley, 118
Irrigation, 25
Iron, 102
Isla Santa, 15
Island of Santa Cruz, 15, 81; illustration island continent, 80
Israel, 134
Israelites, 118
Italy, 13, 19

Jupiter, 115

Kendall, Dr Anne, 92–93
Knossos, 8, 59; Prince of, 70
Knowledge, tree of, 95
Kota Mama, 133–134

La Paz, 121, 124, 127
Landsat, 7
Latitude, 5, 115, 118
Lead, 99, 102, 158
Lebanon, 116
Leucippe, 39
Libya, 9, 15, 19, 33–35, 59, 60, 65, 67
Lima, 99, 102
Longitude, 2, 115
Ludgate, 108
Lunar calendar, 13; months, 13

Ma-gur, 117
Manoa, Lake, 85
Mammoth, 82
Margarita, Isle of, 2
Marinus of Tyre, 107
Mastodons, 20
Maya, 52, 71, 93
Measurement units, 92–94
Medinet Habu, 13
Mediterranean, 11, 13, 51, 53, 60, 62, 68
Melqart, 104
Menes, King, 59
Meridians, 106–107, 109–110, 115
Mesopotamia, 116–118
Metals, 11, 40, 96, 99, 102, 119, 158, 160
Mexica, 73, 76, 78
Mexico, 10, 53, 54, 73–74, 76–77, 81; city, 76; gulf of, 51, 71; lagoon of, 77–78; valley of, 4, 76, 78
Midas, 54
Mile, geographic, 111
Minchin, Lake, 11, 81
Minoans, 62–64, 82
Minotaur, 68
Mississippi, River, 51, 54
Moon, 114–116
Month, sidereal, 68, 114; synodic, 114
Myrine, city, 84; queen, 83

Nahuatl, 4, 10, 75
NASA, 7
Navigation, 2, 53, 115–116
Neith, 31, 60
Nereids, 42
Newton, Sir Isaac, 115
New World, 2, 106
Nile, 31; Delta, 13, 30
Niobe, 31
Noah, 117, 119

North Pole, 81
Nuttal, Zelia, 71

Okeanos, 15
Olmecs, 71, 81
Old World, 106
Ophir, 102
Ordnance Survey, 107
Orichalcum, 11, 19, 21, 42, 159; mines of, 40; pillar of, 47; explanation of, 96–97, 158
Orinoco, River, 85
Oruro, 11, 69, 126–127, 131, 160

Pacific Ocean, 15, 22, 53, 112
Panama, Isthmus of, 75
Paraguay, River, 104
Pareto, Bartolomeo, 2, 3
Paria, Gulf of, 2
Palestine, 14, 53
Pampas, 20
Peacocks, 102–103
Peru, 53, 54, 71, 82, 91, 97, 112; ships of, 112; wealth of, 57, 97–100
Petra, 134
Phaethon, 31
Philip II, 101
Philistines, 14, 65; illustration, 67
Phoenicians, 53, 58, 68, 102, 104, 106, 107, 110, 115, 116, 118–119
Pilcomayo, River, 22, 102, 104, 133, 134
Piri Reis map, 116
Ptolemy, of Alexandria, 107
Pizarro, 57, 98
Plain, 5–6, 44–45, 60, 63–64, 94; description of, 22, 25, 39, 60, 161–162; dimensions of, 5, 44–45, 60, 63, 64, 94; location of, 10, 156, 161; map of, 23–24; on south side, 87–88

Platinum, 97
Plato, 5–6, 29, 61
Plate, River, 2, 102, 117, 118
Plethrum, 41, 45
Pole, 92
Poma, Huaman, 86, 88, 89, 92, 93
Poopo, Lake, 5, 7, 10, 11, 13, 17, 22, 25, 28, 61, 78, 82, 83, 99, 121, 122, 130, 133, 149, 155; cross section, 27; map of, 22, 26
Popul Vuh, 55
Poseidon, 17, 18, 47, 60, 156; dwelling of, 39; grove of, 43; temple to, 21, 42
Potosi, 11, 21, 96, 99, 104, 133, 160; illustration, 101
Pygmalion, 110, 111
Pyramid, the great, 4, 5, 111
Pyrra, 31

Quechua, 4, 83
Quesada, Jiménez de, 84
Quetzalcoatl, 10

Rain, 37, 155
Raleigh, Sir Walter, 85
Rameses, II, 112; III, 13, 14, 58, 65; illustration, 66
Red Sea, 102, 112, 117, 133
Reed ship, 116–117, 133
Rio de la Plata, 22, 102, 104, *see also* River Plate
Roads, Inca, 57, 92
Royal Air Force, 7
Revelations, 94
Round Table, 108

Sacsayhuaman, 91
Sais, 30, 59, 60, 82
Salars, 28; *see* 'Coipasa'; *see* 'Uyuni'
Salt pans, 26
San Salvador, 2

Savoy, Gene, 86, 93
Santorini, 63–64
Sares cycle, 115
Satellite photographs, 137–142, 144, 148; key to, 136
Scilly Isles, 115
Sea Peoples, 13, 65, 67, 68, 112, 116, 119, 154; illustration, 66, 67
Semites, 52, 118
Shusi, 93
Sicily, 62
Siculus, Diodorus, 54, 62, 83, 111
Silver, 11, 21, 38, 42, 54, 57, 64, 97, 99, 102, 104; river of – *see* 'rio de la plata'; silver mountain, 101, 103, 104
Socrates, 29
Solomon, King, 102–103, 119, 133, 143
Solon, 22, 29–38, 59, 61, 62, 69, 82, 93, 156
South Sea, 53, 88
St Pauls Cathedral, 107
Stade, Greek, 5, 12, 20–22, 25, 42, 44–45, 46, 161; explanation of, 94
Stanfords, 7
Stars, 113–115
Stationers' Hall, 131
Stonehenge, 4
Strabo, 111
Straits, 34; *see also* Gibraltar
Sumeria, 116–118; measurements of, 92–93
Superior, Lake, 57
Sykes, Egerton, 131

Tahuantinsuyo, 10, 114; map of, 88–90
Tarija, 133
Tarshish, 102–104, 133
Tauca, Lake, 11, 81, 82
Teide, Mt., 107

Temple, on Atlantis, 42, 44; of Ezekiel, 5, 94,; of Poseidon, 47; of Solomon, 102, 119; of the sun, 114; of Tiahuanaco, 123

Tenochtitlan, 76, 78; illustration, 77

Texcoco, Lake, 76

Thera, 63

Theseus, 36, 68, 154

Thom, Prof Alexander, 93

Tiahuanaco, 1, 73, 83, 123; cross section, 27; statue from, 75

Tigris, River, 118

Timaeus, 9, 29, 59, 61

Tin, 11, 21, 42, 57–58, 64, 96–97, 102, 158

Titicaca, Lake, 1, 2, 10, 12, 17, 22, 83, 86, 116–117, 133; cross section, 27; map of, 23, 26, 146

Tobacco, 112

Toltec, 55, 73

Toledo, 127–128

Trench, 25, 45, 61, 162; *see also* canals; *see also* channels

Trireme, 20, 22, 44

Tritonis, Lake, 82–83

Troy, 8, 65, 68, 84, 154

Tula, 73–74, 123

Tunnels, 98–100; map of, 100

Tuscany, 13, 34, 40

Tyrambel, 53

Tyre, 102, 110; King of, 157 (*see* Hiram)

Ur, 116–117, 119

Uru, 78

Uruk, 116

Uru Uru, Lake, 78, 82, 83, 116, 126

Utu-Nipishtim, 117–118

Uyuni, Salar de, cross section, 27

Venezuela, 2

Vere, Domingo de, 85

Verrill, Hyatt and Ruth, 94

Vespucci, Amerigo, 2

Viracochas, 98

Volcano, 10, 21, 56, 60, 63, 126, 129, 148–150; avenue of, 13

Waldseemuller, Martin, 2

War, 32–34, 48, 61–62, 67

Watling Island, 2

Werner, John, 116

Wolfram, 21

Woolley, Sir Leonard, 118

Wren, Sir Christopher, 107–108

Xerxes, 104

Yard, 93; megalithic, 93

Yukatan, 73

Yukon, 81

Zeus, 37, 49

Zinc, 21, 96, 97, 99, 158